To the
Memory
of
Childhood

To the
Memory
of
Childhood

Lydia
Chukovskaya

Translated by
Eliza Kellogg Klose

Northwestern University Press
Evanston, IL

Northwestern University Press
Evanston, IL 60201

Printed in the United States of America

This translation was funded by the Wheatland Foundation.

Chapters 1, 2, 3, and 4 appeared in slightly different form in *Formations* (Spring-Summer 1987).

Library of Congress Cataloging-in-Publication Data

Chukovskaia, Lidiia Korneevna.
  To the memory of childhood.

  Translation of: Pamiati detstva.
  Includes bibliographies.
  1. Chukovskaia, Lidiia Korneevna—Biography—Youth.
2. Chukovskii, Kornei, 1882-1969—Biography—Family.
3. Authors, Russian—20th century—Biography. I. Title.
PG3476.C485Z47313 1988 891.73'42 [B] 88-12480
ISBN 0-8101-0789-9
ISBN 0-8101-0790-2 (pbk.)

*I, by the way, never seek to
avoid digressions and episodes—
every conversation proceeds that way,
life itself proceeds that way.*

My Past and Thoughts
Alexander Herzen

Contents

Illustrations

All photographs courtesy of Lydia Chukovskya

CHAPTER

I

Back then, when we were children, in Kuokkala, he seemed to us the tallest man on earth. When he went into his study, he had to duck his head to avoid bumping it on the doorjamb. When he set you on his shoulder, you'd be high enough to see through the scattered pine trees to the farthest, farthest reaches of the bay. During a thaw he could easily jump up and hit the icicles hanging off the second-floor balcony with his ski pole, and those which hung from the roof of the woodshed he could manage even without a pole—just reach out his hand and break one off. He was long-armed and long-legged, long and narrow. Who was taller than he? No one! By his length you could measure fences, spruces, pines, waves, people, sheds, trees, heights and depths. His height was given us by fate as a sort of cubit, a natural unit of measurement. Sitting in a boat, trailing our fingers over the side in the transparent gray water, we'd often estimate distances: and if we were calculating the depth, to the very, very bottom—how many papas would it come to: six or more? "Heavens, no! What do you mean, six! It's at least twelve!"

That was out on the water.

In the woods, craning our necks before an enormously tall pine: "This one is probably ten papas from top to bottom!"

He had the feet of a giant: no matter what boots he bought in Vyborg or Petersburg—they never fit; they were too small. Too narrow. Too short. They pinched. They gave him blisters. They had to be taken back to the cobbler again for stretching. If only he could try on that huge, red shoe which hung as an advertisement beneath the sign at the shoemaker's shop by the station. What a shame: that shoe, if it did fit, was intended for a one-footed giant and our giant, praise the good lord, had not one foot but two.

His walk and his behavior were also those of a giant. Not just children, even grown-ups could hardly keep up with him. He would walk along the beach while I trotted along beside him. It took five of my little steps to equal one of his. He dealt with objects in a giantlike way, too: always dragging them off to high places. A hammer or a brush has disappeared—pull up a chair and look on the top of the sideboard or the wardrobe; he left them there on his way by. They were handier for him up there. And what a sneeze he had! Not just people—the whole dacha would shake! And what a spluttering when he washed himself! He'd lather up his cheeks, his chest, his neck and splutter. As if the main thing in washing was the spluttering.

Tall as he was, with his long arms and long legs, he could toss up to the ceiling and catch without a miss a stick, a plate, or one of us. Skinny but strong, he loved fun and he loved to get people with a clever jibe. Restless and carefree, he was always ready to worm his way into our games or invent for us a new one.

At that time Kornei Chukovsky's first children's book was still three years off, his second, almost ten, he had not yet written a single line for children, but he himself, both physically and temperamentally, seemed expressly designed "for younger children" and produced in a special one-of-a-kind edition.

We were lucky. We had been given this one-of-a-kind edition for our own. And, as if understanding his special purpose, we played not just with him but on him, using him as a toy: when he lay on the sand, we climbed on him as on a fallen tree; jumped off his shoulders onto the sofa, as if off the porch onto the grass; walked or crawled through his open legs when he declared them a gate. He was our leader, the commander of our games, our studies, our work, our captain on seagoing excursions, and at the same time our favorite toy. Not a windup toy, but a live one.

Incidentally, although he had not yet written children's books, he was already composing whimsical children's rhymes, just for domestic consumption, easily, on the spur of the moment. At that time he didn't write them down in his thick notebooks as he did later on, he didn't combine them into poems and longer pieces, work and rework them for months, even years, before handing them over to the publisher, or read them in schools, kindergartens, hospitals and large lecture halls with white columns. These were improvisations, domestic impromptus, one-day creations—nothing more.

> . . . Lidauchek,
> Best of all daaauughters!

he would say to me in an ingratiating, singsong, somehow long voice. (I was still so little and silly, I couldn't guess why I should be called "little rider."* Was I really riding on something?)

Or he'd growl gaily, stamping on me with his giant feet:

---

*The Russian phrase "iz dochek" (of daughters), if pronounced quickly, sounds like "yezdochek" (little rider). (Translator)

Oh, you nasty little girl!
Ho-ow you make my stomach whirl!

"Papa," I'd say, shifting impatiently from one foot to the other, under-standing that he wanted to play with me no less than I with him, "Papa! Put me up on the cupboard."

He'd take a step back. Look down threateningly at me from his great height. Bend down and waggle his long finger in front of my nose.

"How many times do I have to tell you! Ask me properly."

The game has begun. I thirst for the ordeal and the terror: the scarier, the better, so that it will all work out in the end. More than anything I am terri-fied of heights, and therefore I ask to be taken not just anywhere, but to the very highest place, right under the ceiling, the top of the cupboard.

"De-ee-ee-ply res-pec-ted, Papa!" I say, syllable by syllable as this game requires. "Place me, if-you-please, on top of the cupboard!"

"Oh ho!" The finger disappears. "And you won't ask to get down?"

"No."

"So, you want to live your whole life on top of the cupboard?"

"On top of the cupboard forever."

He lifts me under the arms, swings me back and forth a minute, sets me on top of the cupboard, and then immediately strides out of the room. To make it even more frightening, he closes the door behind him.

I sit there, terrified. As if not mine, my poor legs hang over the precipice. I peek down into the abyss. There, way below, is the yellow linoleum with its black pattern. I'll fall and break into bits like a teacup. Why did I ever ask to be put up on the cupboard? Never again will I run on the beach, sit down with everyone at the lunchtable . . . Everyone's swimming, playing tag, and he's with them . . . and I? I have to live on top of the cupboard. Never, never again will I throw flat stones into the water, counting how many times they skip, and never again will he call me to build a dam in our brook!

"Papa!"

Silence.

"Papa!"

No answer. He's gone, he's forgotten about me and left me here for-ever . . .

If I look down, fear overwhelms me. Up is no better. There's the ceiling, the very height of heights. He is teaching us not to be afraid, Kolya and me. He tells us to climb branching pine trees. Higher! Higher! Still higher! But then he stands under the tree and directs us and we can hold on to his voice.

I sit, frozen with fear, glancing at my useless feet. All alone.

"Deeply respected, Papa," I try again, without hope, "please, take me down from the cupboard. I don't like living here. Please!"

His steps! He's here! He only pretended to go far away! He comes in, takes me up under the arms, swings me, tosses me about a bit, and then

3

sets me down on the floor. What happiness! I am once again on the floor with everybody else, I can run wherever I wish.

You can trust his hands completely. They always catch you in time, never drop you or hurt you. True, those hands could never tie the hood under my chin, fasten cuff links, cook fried eggs, iron a shirt or pack a suitcase. Such long, flexible fingers—yet these things were beyond them. But throwing me or my younger brother Boba almost to the ceiling, or flinging us both on the sofa to see how high the springs would bounce us—that they can do with ease. Flying or falling, don't be afraid; they will always catch you and hold you. And then torture! Our favorite game. Unscrewing-the-ears. Chopping-off-the-head. Sawing-in-half (side of the hand across the stomach). Thumps-on-the-rump. Pulling-out-of-hair... Those big, reliable hands, full of fun, with their round, shining clean nails. And even in the coldest weather, hot as can be.

...Here we are, returning from the station along the Big Road. We'd gone together to the post office. The temperature, thirty below.* On both sides empty dachas, their frozen boards crackling like gunfire in the cold; flower-beds buried in snow; fenceposts drowning in the snow. Snow, and more snow along the edge of the Big Road, but down the middle, crystalline bright, runs the hard, endless track, packed down by sleighs and trampled by hooves. The frost hangs in the air like an invisible barrier. Why is it that snow is called white, when in fact it is dark blue, pink, many-colored, sparkling? But today the snow doesn't make me happy. I'm freezing. My lips, brows, and forehead are freezing. Even my teeth. And my feet? I simply don't have any feet. But he doesn't even notice the cold. He's actually hot. His coat is thrown open, his hands are mittenless, the earflaps on his sheep-skin hat, untied. Though I'm all wrapped up, I begin to cry from the cold. I'm shivering as though I were in a summer dress, not a fur coat, hood, scarf and leggings. I cry quietly at first, then louder and louder, and the hot tears make me feel even colder. He takes me in his arms, takes off my frozen boots and puts them in one pocket, then puts both my feet in the other along with his hot hand.

It's crowded. A happy crowdedness.

In a minute, held tight in his palm, my frozen toes and heels come back to life. Infused by his inexhaustible warmth, they warm through and through, grow hot, just as if we were already at home and I were perched in the dining room by the white tile stove with birch coals smouldering splendidly in its square maw.

Thus he carries me through the frost along the road: both my feet snuggled into his pocket under his huge, hot hand.

---

*Celsius; about -22°F. Temperatures throughout are Celsius. (Translator)

4

CHAPTER

II

When we were at Kuokkala, he did all the manual labor around the house himself—carried water, chopped wood, lit the stove. Working as yardman as well as kitchen help, he scattered puddles with a broom, cleared ice off the porch steps with a crowbar, or shoveled snow off the walk from the porch to the gate with a square wooden shovel, making a narrow passage between the snowdrifts. We went along behind him with little shovels. Walking in the deep channel, we'd smooth the sides with our shovels; if we touched the snow of the wall, we could feel it prickle even through our woolen gloves.

At some point during his impoverished youth in Odessa, he had worked with a housepainters' cooperative and developed a lifelong passion for transforming an old, dilapidated fence into a new, well-cared-for one with the help of a paintbrush. There was something festive about this work. The appetite with which he painted a fence or a box, stirring his brush around in the thick, green paint, would have made Tom Sawyer's comrades envious. It certainly made us envious. And just like Tom Sawyer, he would indulgently allow us to try that rare treat, fencepainting. One long stroke of green on the wooden gate.

"Here before me stand, and do as I command."

He would hand me the brush with all the ceremony of a king offering the scepter to his heir apparent.

"Hold it straight! Don't drip! Don't drip! O-o-o, I'm very fierce when I'm angry!"

His hands, which could never tie a tie or sew on a button, were perfectly adapted for rough, manual labor whether it was shoveling snow off the roof or sawing up a log; and strange as it seems, though he couldn't thread a needle, he had a magician's skill at sleight of hand. Fitting a cuff link into his shirt sleeve was impossible for him, but making magic with a saltshaker—no problem. He'd place the saltshaker full of salt on his palm and with a sudden dip of his hand describe a half circle in the air; as if pinned in place, the saltshaker would not fall nor, miraculously, would any of the salt spill.

So much for the saltshaker! Even chairs obeyed him.

A chair would balance obediently on his outstretched index finger for two minutes. The juggler would twist, dance, and bend to keep the chair from falling, and thanks to all the twisting and turning, the chair would not tip over but stand straight, one leg on his index finger.

And then there was his stick. A short, thick club. He would throw it and catch it, throw it and catch it, faster, faster, faster; it would turn in the air like the fat spoke of a wheel, then he'd throw it suddenly to my older brother Kolya or some startled guest, telling them not to duck but to catch it in flight and throw it back. Then he'd stand as if waiting for a blow, straightening his narrow shoulders and sticking out his chest. "Here's my chest. Go ahead and hit me!" But no one could strike him: his long arm would reach out and grasp the stick a mere yard from his chest, then throw it back at his opponent.

He rowed, swam, dove, and skied, moving energetically in the fresh air, at work or at play, amidst waves, sand, children, and pine trees.

He loved and respected play in a remarkable way, not drawing a sharp line between what was work and what was play. He tried to draw us children into every kind of work, turning any job into a game. Indoors or out.

Our little piece of property was hardly a garden; it was more like a copse of spruce and pine, similar to many others in Kuokkala. On two sides it was set off from our neighbors by a fence, on the third, by a brook; the fourth side, the seashore, needed no marker. Our pine trees ran freely up to the yellow sand, at the edge of which was a row of rough, round stones, sometimes covered with froth, sometimes dry and pleasantly sun-warmed. In the heat of summer, the ground was slippery beneath the firs; there were spruce and pine needles, stumps and cones, and snakelike roots on which we constantly bloodied our bare feet. The wood was like any other wood; the only real garden was near the porch—a single flowerbed, two gravel paths, and a row of nasturtiums along the edge of the veranda.

The wood was like any other, but despite its small size, it gave Kornei Ivanovich plenty of trouble.

It had to be defended against two sorts of incursions: the gradual, insidious ones of the brook, and the violent ones of the sea.

In this defense, we also took part.

The brook had the habit of slyly, bit-by-bit washing away the earth from under the pines. When Kornei Ivanovich discovered the damage, he was in a frenzy to staunch the wound, hauling on his back bag after bag of sand from the seashore just like a real stevedore, and we would scurry along behind him with watering can, pail or kitchen pot. At his command—"One, two, three, close your eyes, p-ou-r!" all the sand would pour out into the water.

A dam of sand was enough to stop the depredations of the brook; but even stones couldn't keep out the sea.

Every fall, in preparation for the storms to come, he'd fish out of the sea with a boathook ten or so woven baskets washed over from Kronstadt (each was big enough to hold Kolya, Boba, and me together) and set them in a row along the pines, hoping to protect the land from the inevitable attack of the waves; with his own hands he would fill every one of the baskets to the brim with stones, by no means an easy task: it took dozens of trips from the water to the basket and back again.

I can see him now: he walks across the sand barefoot, in rolled up trousers, hands above his lowered head, in each hand a huge, heavy rock. He carefully watches his step to avoid stumbling; once a rock fell out of his hand and nearly broke his foot.

We walk behind him, also carrying stones, even small Boba. We also keep our eyes on the ground.

He stops in front of the baskets, waiting for us. Rocks above our heads, we gather round.

"Throw!" he shouts. What a lovely crash as the rocks land in the basket! For the joy of that crash we toiled and carried...Now was that work or play?

Words like "sport" and "competition" we never heard from him, but he taught us how to ski, how to sled on Finnish sleds, called *potkukelke*, how to row and how to swim. We were as comfortable on skis as in felt boots or gloves: we'd step out onto the porch and right into our bindings.

He was an expert at the ancient games of boating, skiing, sledding, even ice-sailing.

I remember that he was the only one in the neighborhood who knew how to fly under sail across the frozen expanse of the sea on those alarming winter days when great green patches of ice sparkled on the wind-scoured bay. The wind would drive the lawless butterfly across the bay to the terror of the horses dragging heavy carts of ice just broken out of holes in the surface. The horses would shy off the track, nearly tipping out the blocks of greenish crystal, and the cartmen, clutching their reins, would shake their fists for a long time at that unexpected sail, borne along who knew where by the wind.

It really was a marvel: a human being standing on some sort of special skis with short steel runners under each foot; he'd stand, holding sticks attached behind his back which supported a square of stretched canvas. And standing, he'd fly.

On days when the wind was especially strong, Kornei Ivanovich would attach the sail not to his skis but to the *potkukelke*. We'd sit on the sled: Kolya and he with me or Boba on his lap. When, after gulping in the stinging cold, we'd return from the open shore to our tree-enclosed yard, surrounded by pine and spruce, it felt stuffy even at twenty below. Every vein had been thoroughly bathed and renewed by the intense cold. But among the pines it felt stuffy. We quickly untied our hood strings, unhooked our collars, shoved our gloves in our pockets. Like him, in these moments we scorned the cold: who could call today cold—it's a scorcher!

He could do anything for us—even, effortlessly, turn freezing cold to warmth.

CHAPTER

III

In the summer our favorite job was going to get water at Repin's house, Penates.

The water from our own well was all right for doing laundry, watering flowers, or washing, but not for drinking. For drinking water we had to go to Penates, where there was an artesian well.

"Let's go!"—and the job (or game?) had begun.

I would run to the shed for the carrying stick. Kolya would have already got the pail and started banging on it. Boba, who understood everything we said but wouldn't yet say a word himself, would grab the end of the stick first for fear we might go without him. Within seconds our Finnish friends Matti, Pavka, and Ida would appear.

Kornei Ivanovich described these trips to Repin's for water many years later in his book *From Two to Five*. But at the time he was simply one of us—lanky and darkly unshaven, wearing old trousers, cheerfully turning up clouds of warm dust with his bare feet, with every bit as much pleasure as we.

We'd arrive at the carved gates of Penates. Opening them without a sound, he'd pucker his lips and in a loud, whistling whisper command us to be quiet. Repin was working; we must maintain complete silence. Even before reaching the gate, at the very beginning of Repin's fence, he'd shush not just us, but the unwary passerby as well. Once inside the gate—total silence. He led us virtually on tiptoe, angrily turning around at the slightest rustle. He could almost shake you behind his back if you made a noise.

It wasn't easy to keep quiet, but the tension of trying heightened the fun: it was as though we had to steal the water from Repin, not just come get it.

Without a sound he hung the pail on the round neck of the tap, then took it off and stood it on the coarse gravel. Now it was our turn. We put our stick through the handle of the heavy pail, and not taking our eyes off the rocking water—don't spill, don't spill—reverently lifted it.

"Shhh! Shhh! Shhh!" demanded our commander in his whistling whisper.

Once again he silently opened and closed the carved gates. At last we'd

reach the end of the fence, and then all our pent-up noise would triumphantly explode.

Since we were all of different heights, the carrying stick banged uncom-
fortably against our legs and sides and the water kept spilling out, but that
didn't bother us. On the way home from Penates we'd shout out the jingle
we'd long ago composed for the occasion and which seemed to grow more
fun with every repetition:

> Two stumps,
> Two root clumps
> Past the fence, then
> Past the jumps—
> Mustn't let the pail be smashed,
> Mustn't let the pail be splashed . . .

Expectantly, we fall silent. The wait seems long, though it actually lasts
only a moment.

"Blyahms!" he shouts.

At the command we lower the bucket to the ground and flop down next
to it.

He flops down with us.

Boba looks into the water, astonished at the way it bends and crinkles his
face.

"March!" shouts our leader. "Quick as a wink!"

Once again we strike up our water-bearers' song, waiting for that blessed
"blyahms!"

With him we could always expect magical amusement.

Whatever you did with him was such fun you couldn't tear yourself away.
Especially the words: "Let's make a trip."

Whether it was a trip to the post office to send off a manuscript, to the
seashore, to Penates to get water, to the shop at the station, to the ends of
the earth, or to go swimming—it didn't matter, as long as you could go with
him.

His only real threat to us as children was "I won't take you with me."
"Tomorrow I won't take you with me." Where he wouldn't take you didn't
matter. That he wouldn't take you with him was what counted. He'd leave
you at home. He'd go away without you. Everyone would be with him, all
together—and you'd be all alone. Without his step, his voice, his hand, his
smile. Sit in the garden and pretend to read. Glance over at the gate and listen: wait 'til you hear voices coming along the lane from the Big Road, then
closer and closer would come his voice, sounding above all the rest, high-
pitched, with a bit of a whistle and whisper, both commanding and mocking.

Happily, though he was hot-tempered, he did not bear grudges. He almost never fulfilled that dire threat, "I won't take you with me tomorrow." He would forget it, and we would be together once more on a trip or at work.

When supplies ran out at home (our parents went into the city very rarely), a whole crowd of us would walk down the Big Road either to the Kuokkala Station or in the other direction—to the Ollila Station, to Killstrom's store, and although the road was totally ordinary, if we went with him instead of Nanny Tonya, the most amazing things would happen in a mile and a half! What he wouldn't conjure up!

He might notice, for instance, that Boba, having silently persuaded us to take him with us, was tiring from the heat, fatigue, and the pound of nuts he was carrying.

"Oh, sorrow!" Kornei Ivanovich would suddenly cry out in a high voice. "My nose has become glued. I can't move. I'm done for! Help! Save me!"

All hunched over, he would fidget about with his nose on the trunk of a tree at the side of the road. His outstretched arms would flail in the air, fingers wiggling helplessly. And his nose—his nose was now unmoving, firmly stuck to the tree. His feet were rooted to the ground. It was all over. Our father was glued there forever.

"Take hold of me and pull! Bobochka! You are my only hope!"

Forgetting his fatigue instantly, Boba grabs him by the knee. Kolya and I each take hold of a long, flailing arm, the tail of his jacket, or Boba's belt. Pull as hard as we can, we cannot budge him. His nose is firmly stuck to the tree, his legs are rooted like tree trunks. For a long time we pull and pull. Occasionally Boba manages to move one of those huge legs just a little, so he doesn't give up hope. But where to! Once again it roots itself. Then, a sudden jolt, and we all fly to the ground: the giant is free. Straightening himself and tossing his head, he holds out a grateful hand to each of us in turn. He offers special thanks to Boba:

"Thank you, Bobochka, you pulled harder than anyone. If it hadn't been for you, I might never have seen my home again."

And Boba continues merrily on his way.

When I began to whimper and fall behind, he would get me going again in a different way. He'd start telling me stories about when I was a baby. They used to wash me in a washtub set up on two stools, and one time the washtub fell over with me in it. At first I cried, then fell quiet. I lay under the washtub without making a sound. Everyone thought I was dead. Fearfully they lifted the tub to look.

"Even you were afraid I was lying there dead?" I asked.

"Even I. 'After all I am somewhat related to you.' "[1]

"And then?"

"And then I lifted the tub . . ."

"And I was alive!" I'd shout with delight. "I was lying there alive and I wasn't crying!"

I wanted him to tell how Mama had hugged me to her and everyone rejoiced, embracing and kissing me, but his mocking nature didn't permit him to dwell on tenderness.

"I was little, but I didn't cry," I prompted. "I'd hurt myself badly, but I didn't cry."

"We cried instead," he broke in. "How you tried our patience." Here he put his hand on my shoulder. "Washing your hair—what a hollering! Soap had got in your eyes . . . There you were all chubby, red and eyebrowless—Phoo! . . . Kolya, by the way, what's the word for 'eyebrows' in English?"

I understood, of course, that he was joking, but there was another story I loved even more than the one about the washtub: that was the one about the way poets had celebrated my birth in verse.

Papa, Mama, and Kolya were living at that time in Petersburg on Kolomensky Street. Mama had gone to a hospital nearby, on the same street, and had returned with me. The poet Sergei Gorodetsky came to congratulate my parents, and on the very threshold of Mama's bedroom had written:

> O, fortune smiles now on the clan Chukovsky,
> They've borne a daughter, lovelier than the rest.

(After this story, so I wouldn't think too much of myself, Kornei Ivanovich nicknamed me "Lovelier." "Tell us, Lovelier, what's 'horseback rider' in English?" "Lovelier, run and tell Boba it's time for dinner.")

In addition to Gorodetsky, it turned out that Valery Bryusov had also praised me in verse.

I could listen with endless delight to the story of how, right after I was born, Valery Yakovlevich Bryusov had sent Kornei Ivanovich a letter enclosing a poem he'd submitted to a Petersburg magazine. If the editor didn't like the poem, added the poet, "I offer it to your newborn daughter for her dowry."[2]

"That was me!" I'd cry. "That was for me!"

And then Kornei Ivanovich, usually responding that "I was now not dowryless," would recite the poem with particular singsong emphasis on the "ee" sound:

> NEar the wEavey, winding NIle, there, where lies
> > the Lake MerIda,
> > and rules the brightly shining Ra,
> There you long ago did love mE, as OsIris loved IsIda,
> > My friend,
> > my sister and my Tsar!
> And the pYramid's penumbra fell upon us from afar.[3]

"Lidka-pyramidka!" shouted Kolya.

"And the pYramid's penumbra fell upon y-o-u from afar!" Kornei Ivanovich would repeat wickedly.

. . . Today we were lucky: after the glued nose, a new adventure, an automobile. Not as usual behind a fence or at a distance, but right close up. We came face-to-face with its glass, its black shininess, its blinding globes of light and deafening horn. Racing towards us with a brilliance even the dust could not dim came a black, glass-and-metal wonder. It flew past. Ordinarily, when we were at home and heard it approaching on the Big Road, there would be no trace of it by the time we had climbed the fence and run across the field: nothing except a cloud of dust up ahead and tire tracks on the road. But luck was with us today: it came flying to meet us as we were walking along the road, and with a roar whizzed past so close you could reach out and touch it; by the time the other children in the neighborhood managed to climb over their fences or run through their gates, we were already down on our haunches examining the "herringbones," the two long tire tracks it left behind.

"Don't breathe, you'll blow away the herringbone," Kolya says to me.

I try not to breathe.

Then all of a sudden, danger looms, a danger so great we forget all about the herringbone.

An enormous dog is running, unchained, back and forth along the fence, barking loudly.

Naturally, we know all the neighbor dogs, both Finnish and Russian, including Repin's one-eyed poodle Mik, but we've never seen this dog before. It probably belongs to some dacha owner, and as a rule we can't stand the dachniks. We consider ourselves locals. We don't run off to Petersburg at the very first sign of autumn's rains and storms. We can do everything the local kids can do: penknife games, marbles, skiing in the winter, rowing, swimming, and going barefoot in the summer; we even understand some Finnish and say a few words like "let's go swimming!" or "rain," and dachniks don't understand a single word—but, worst of all, they are afraid of everything. Go barefoot? Not allowed, you might catch cold. Play with knives? Not allowed, you might cut yourself. Go swimming? Not allowed! Ay-ay-ay, you might drown. Not allowed! They are so afraid of the sea that one time when our captain invited a little girl from a dacha to come on our boat with us and said to her: "You sit on the bottom," she thought he meant sit on the bottom of the sea. She cried until we turned back to shore and he carried her to the arms of her governess. To their way of thinking, lots of things aren't nice. Swimming in your underwear—not nice. One should wear bathing suits. Climbing fences and trees—not nice. Playing with the Finnish children—not nice. . . And is it nice to have a guard dog for your dacha so fierce that it tries to throw itself at any innocent passerby?

13

Dachniks are cowards. They are afraid of everything, most of all of being robbed. And so they'd brought a guard dog with them.

But this time we were the cowards, not they.

Past the magnificent flower garden, past the three-story dacha, along the newly painted fence, then back again, barking horribly, runs the dog. It's looking for a way to get through the fence and come bite us. What does it think we are? Some kind of thieves planning to steal its flowers! We walk hurriedly along the fence with our packages. He takes the lead. We want to run, not walk. He won't let us. The most important thing, he says in a quiet voice, is not-to-run. We must do exactly as he does. If only he'd say: one, two, three! Go!

Look out! The dog didn't find a hole to crawl through so it's digging one itself. The dirt sprays out behind its flying paws.

Damned fence! How long it is! If only we could just run past it at top speed—but we can't.

The dog is out!

"Throw down your bags!" he shouts.

Throw we do. Into the dry ditch at the side of the road go the candy, cookies, sugar, soap . . .

With bounding leaps the dog charges toward us. It's more tiger than dog! . . .

Oh, how I want to run! I seize him by one hand, Boba takes the other.

"One, two, three! Do exactly as I do!"

He pushes our hands away and drops to all-fours in the dust.

We follow suit right next to him.

The whole family is down on their knees: he, Boba, Kolya, and I, plus Matti, Ida, and Pavka.

"Ruf, ruf, ruf!" he barks.

We're not surprised. The dog is surprised to death.

"Ruf, ruf, ruf," we join in.

Just as if we'd thrown a stone at it, the dog tucks its tail between its legs and runs away. It's probably the first time in its life the dog has seen four-footed humans. We go on barking for a long time—long after he has risen to his feet, smoothing his trousers, and the dog has crawled back under the fence and taken refuge on the green porch.

It takes him some time to quiet us. Seems it's a lot of fun to bark at a dog!

CHAPTER

IV

"The skinny housekeeper of the famous bald traveler, who was suffering from scarlet fever, ate the fried eggs which she'd prepared for her curly haired niece. Jumping onto the angry stallion, the long-awaited guest, urging the horse on with a poker, tore off to the stable..."

That was my assignment. I was to translate it into English by tomorrow. He had created the nonsense especially for me; for Kolya—a different, equally nonsensical assignment; he created his amusing texts using the English words he'd given us to learn the day before.

I was six or seven; Kolya, nine or ten. We would translate similar nonsense by the yard and delight in it. What squeals of laughter! "Urging the horse on with a poker!"

Our teacher tried to turn even our lessons into a game. He succeeded partially.

"The spotted butterfly, hatching out of a chicken's egg, fell right into the old bachelor's plate..."

A butterfly from a chicken's egg! We loved translating. But memorizing the words—that was another story. He tested us on them regularly, and to our way of thinking, most inconveniently. We'd be in the boat or on our way to the post office or Penates and he'd suddenly toss questions at us: what's "headlight" in English? What's "drugstore"? "Tell me, Kolechka," he'd say in a gentle but slightly threatening voice, "what's 'straw' in English? Hmm. That's right... And Lidauchek, can you tell me what 'the star' means? How do you say many stars? Louder! I can't hear you... And how would you say 'happy'? And how about 'underbrush'? and what's a 'spoon'?"

Both Russian to English and English to Russian.

He would thrust a stick in our hands and ask us to write English words in the snow or in the sand. He would ask us to write the words he'd given us earlier that morning in his study. At random. In order. Every other word. Old words. New words.

In his younger days he couldn't control his hot temper—if we hadn't learned our words well he would strike the table with his fist and send us out of the room or—worst of all!—lock the offender in the storeroom.

Nothing gamelike about that. That was plain disgust.

"Get out!" he would shout at me when I answered hesitantly or slowly. "You've been loafing, lying around in bed! I've been at my desk since five o'clock this morning."

(He, in fact, often worked round-the-clock at his desk, and idleness in others aroused his wrathful contempt. If he saw us lolling about with nothing to do, he would immediately find a job for us: covering textbooks with colored paper, arranging the books on the shelves in his study in order of size, weeding the flowerbeds, or, with the windows open, clapping the dust off his big books. Anything so we wouldn't just hang around wasting time.)

Our lack of passion for learning English stumped and irritated him. He took it personally.

When he shouted at me for not learning my English words well enough, I would hide in my favorite hiding place, in the bushes behind the icehouse, to cry and study the words all over again. With a sympathetic sigh, Boba would hold out to me on his outstretched palm three blackberries and a huckleberry.

Once Kolya had to sit for a whole hour in the storeroom, all because of his English words. Not because he hadn't studied them at all, no, he'd studied them, but not well enough. In the eyes of our teacher that was a crime. The day before Kolya hadn't known the English word for "spoon," today he'd known the word but spelled it incorrectly.

He simply couldn't stand knowing things halfway, doing things in a half-baked fashion.

In one of his English books, which sits to this day on the shelf of the dacha outside Moscow, the following sentence is underlined in red: "Whatever load he was called upon to pull, he pulled with the force of four horses in a single harness." He worked like that his whole life. And that's what he expected from us. But we . . . what about us! His idea of learning an English word was to know it at any moment, in any context, in all its forms. But we! Today we knew it, tomorrow not, we recognized it in the singular—in the plural, not always. Insufficient desire, apathy instead of enthusiasm. Passivity instead of noble, eager passion. "You shirkers!"

He'd spent his own childhood and adolescence in Odessa in lower-middle-class surroundings where people didn't read. Every book he'd read, he'd had to get hold of by himself, and entirely on his own try to read and understand it.

But we . . . Our house was full of books, both Russian and English, and we were slugabeds who tried to slip away whenever he quizzed us on our words. He had had no one to teach him. We had a tutor who came to our

16

house to help Kolya prepare for gymnasium, and he himself was happy to work with us any time he was free. And we, what did we do but memorize as quickly as possible, instead of delighting in each new English word and throwing ourselves into our books as he had.

He had been forced to leave school in the fifth grade because of Delyanov's law against education for "cooks' children" (partly because he was born out-of-wedlock, but mostly because his mother, our grandmother Ekaterina Osipovna, had had to support herself by working as a laundress). Everything he knew, he knew from books and had learned on his own, without teachers or tutors, by the force of his intellect and will alone; by himself he had crossed one of the most impassable of all barriers, the threshold between the petty bourgeoisie and the intelligentsia. All his life he was affected by the diffidence and pride of the self-taught man: an exaggerated modesty before people better educated than he, and a modest pride at his own knowledge, won as it was against all odds.

The family of his schoolmate Boris Zhitkov were the first members of the intelligentsia whom he ever met. He'd been twelve or thirteen at the time. They played the piano and the violin. The house was full of books, atlases, maps; the children even had their own microscope . . . In his memoirs, Kornei Ivanovich writes that the head of the family and each of its members had a most extraordinary attribute: not only did they love books themselves, they also loved to share them with others. The very first time he met them they lent him *Don Quixote.*

"I knew nothing about anything," says he, writing about his adolescence.[1]

But how he wanted to learn! The more and the sooner, the better.

When he was young, working as best he could on his own, he had studied English and had been astonished and delighted translating Walt Whitman and reading Thackeray's *Vanity Fair.* At age twenty-one he'd gone to London as correspondent for an Odessa newspaper; there he sat from morning till night in the library of the British Museum, studying and making up for lost time.

"I sit at my books in a frenzy," he wrote in 1904 from London to his young wife in Odessa. "I study words endlessly (not so very many anymore), I read in bed, at the table, on the street. I get to the museum between nine and ten in the morning and leave after the closing bell . . . Everything I do, I do for you so that when we meet again, I can tell you about it and teach you."

And then he sent her a list of words from a book by Carlyle: "Study the words first, then read the book."

There was a whole glossary for Thackeray's *Vanity Fair:* "My God . . . how I wish you knew English so you could read *Vanity Fair* with the same ease and pleasure as I."[2]

The method of learning ten words a day, which he had developed at some point for himself, then used to teach our mother, he now used with us children.

He wanted to awake passion and zeal in us, to cultivate in us a thirst for learning. But we! Unlike him, we didn't want to read "in bed, at the table, on the street." Not enthusiasm, but apathy. We stuck to the minimum: just the words we were given. Not one word more.

"Get out of here!" he cried when it turned out Kolya knew his words but didn't remember how to spell them. "Nonentity!" (That was one of his favorite insults.) "To the storeroom! Sit there and stare at the ceiling where I don't have to look at you! Go ahead and die an idler!"

We didn't have to search for anything. Struggle for anything. It wasn't our lot to sit half-starved on a scorching hot roof practicing our English words in spackle while waiting for the painters to arrive, or to study English literature in a library, without a bite to eat from early morning until closing time. Everything was at our disposal: all we had to do was put out a hand, and there was a book. In our own house, in his study (which seemed small because one half of it was taken up with a huge sofa, the other with his desk), on two walls, from floor to ceiling, on the desk and on the windowsill, lying and standing, there were books.

Russian and English.

(They were in good order, but a lively, working order, not a dead one: they were neat, without grease spots, bent pages, or dust, but there were notes aplenty; reading to him meant becoming familiar with, judging and arguing with an author; as a result there were columns of numbers all over the inside cover—page numbers—and the pages themselves would be covered with notes and underlinings. Further, inveterate editor that he was, he ʹ considered every book, his own or someone else's, a manuscript, not yet complete and subject to refinement: he couldn't resist correcting a typographical error, a clumsy turn of phrase, or an author's error.)

The windows of his study looked out over the neighboring peasant's meadow, which lay on the other side of the fence: in the summer it was all bluebells, daisies and clover, in the winter, a smooth blanket of snow. Books stood on their shelves, classic and contemporary alike. The Russian books (except the classics) were mostly autographed copies or marked "for review only": prose writers, poets, or newspaper editors sent them to the critic Kornei Chukovsky. He had brought many of the English books back from London with him and he was always ordering new ones. From my earliest childhood I remember Walt Whitman in numerous editions, Milton, Shakespeare, Keats, Swinburne, Grey, Browning, Byron, Shelley, and Burns next to Zhukovsky, Pushkin, Batyushkov, Baratynsky, Nekrasov, Polonsky, Lermontov, Fet, Tyutchev, and Blok.

Queen of them all, however, no matter where we lived, was the *Encyclo-*

pedia Britannica. In Kuokkala it sat resplendent in green next to the gray Vengherov edition of Pushkin.

Encyclopedia Britannica was his lifelong teacher—a sort of personal portable British Museum library in book form.

He never complained about his path, the difficult path of self-education, quite to the contrary, he asserted that if a man thirsted for knowledge he could attain it, so long as he had books—and will power. Furthermore, he was convinced that knowledge gained through one's own efforts and choice was more sound and productive than that learned arbitrarily from others. That's why he rejoiced so at our pleasure in translation and grieved so at our lack of interest in studying our words. He taught us English in a most elementary way toward a most elementary end: to have us read and understand what was read to us in the fastest way possible. Certainly, he taught us English because he loved English literature and because he had worked so hard on it himself, but most of all, it was because he wanted to give us yet another key to knowledge. He didn't care a bit about our pronunciation or our ability to speak freely in English: if we should have the chance to live among English-speaking people, he explained, we could learn that in two weeks. Read, read, read! Learn words! Here are the words from Oscar Wilde's "The Happy Prince," and here are those from a page of *Oliver Twist* by Dickens. Translating, now, that was a good game.

He was totally indifferent to the work we were doing to get ready for the gymnasium. He signed our weekly gradebooks virtually without looking at them, considering both the grades and his signature mere formalities. He did not believe that teachers in the state schools were capable of inspiring children, and learning without inspiration he considered to be worthless. Having noticed that Kolya was interested in geography as a young child, he brought him a new atlas almost every time he went to Petersburg, and when he went to London in 1916, he brought back so many maps there wasn't wall space for them all. And catching Kolya's enthusiasm, he would crawl with him across a map spread out on the floor . . . I was pitifully lacking in any talent for arithmetic. Having determined that I had no aptitude for mathematics whatsoever, that no matter how much energy I expended on problems and examples, I'd end up with tears not answers, he began to solve my problems for me and shamelessly give them to me to copy, to the utter horror of our tutor.

"The multiplication tables and the four basic operations are enough for her!" he said. "She'll only be eight once. There's no point burdening a mind with what it rejects. At no other age is perception so fresh or memory so good . . . Okay, Lovelier, recite me 'The Lay of Wise Oleg' . . ."

I recited. My mind did not reject poetry. It was harder for me to forget a poem than to remember it.

. . . Basically, we loved our English lessons. If only it hadn't been for those lists of words! Although once you managed to get the words, then the fun began:

"The old maid, having stuffed herself with putty, fell into the pond. The strong south wind drove her right onto the cliff. But at that moment a swallow flew to her and seized hold of her hair."

Having stuffed herself with putty! What fun! Simple things pleased us and we laughed uproariously.

Then, after the silly nonsense, we would open our Dickens to the page for which he'd prepared us, and all by ourselves, without his help, we'd be able to figure out what happened next to Oliver Twist—oh! that joy made learning the words, even suffering his displeasure, all worthwhile.

That was even better magic than the saltshaker.

CHAPTER V

He taught us how to play chess and checkers (at one time, in London, he'd been an avid chess player), how to play charades and put on plays (he wrote one, *The Pot-bellied Tsar*, just for us), how to build castles and dams in the sand, how to solve chess problems; he prompted games—who could jump highest, who could walk farthest along the top of the fence or railroad track, who could best hide the ball or himself; he played skittles with us or hopped on one foot to the gate and back. He turned cleaning up the desk into our favorite game: what fun it was to pull out the blotter tacks with the special little forked metal tool, lay down new green paper, then tack it smoothly and evenly in place; to wipe out the drawers with the special rag he kept hidden away, and then, at his command, run to the creek and wash it with gray soap from a special hiding place! What fun to hang the rag over a pine tree branch and carefully check—was it dry yet? To sneak a touch of the tiny, shaggy rag all covered with dark blue inkspots on which he wiped his pens! (The ink wipe was the daughter of the big dust cloth...) He eagerly joined our ordinary, everyday children's games, "I Spy," races, snowball fights, even roughhousing: all of a sudden there'd be a loud guffaw, a great squashing, a pile of bodies on the floor, and squeals... He asked us riddles and had us make up our own to ask Boba.

Only one game was out of the question in our house, as unthinkable as, say, ripping someone open—that was cards.

He knew that Pushkin, Tolstoy, and Nekrasov all played cards, but that didn't make a bit of difference.

To him cards and the plague were one and the same. Absolutely no card-playing under his roof! Poor Nanny Tonya,* who loved reading the future in cards, had to hide her pack at the very bottom of her trunk.

---

*The Russian nanny (nyanya) was a simple peasant woman whose primary responsibility was the children but who also took on many other household chores. (Translator)

21

Was he afraid of arousing in us a passion for games of chance? Scarcely; he was the one who made everything exciting. After all, "Black Petka"* or dominoes were scarcely less dangerous in this regard than cards, yet these games he played with us. But cards were taboo; a pack of cards probably conjured up for him an image of green tables, betting chalks, soiled ruble notes, and an idle, lounging, good-for-nothing Kolya dealing out the game. A badly brought up Kolya! A Kolya without a taste for intellectual life or hard work! To his mind cards were the mark of the enemy. Although in every time and every place people have played cards, he associated them with only one place, Odessa, and only one time—a time of humiliation!—his boyhood and adolescence, and that narrow-minded, vulgar circle of shopkeepers and clerks for whom his mother worked. He saw the people who despised his mother, his sister and himself; the world which took pleasure in excluding "cook's children" from gymnasium education, the world which he (its *"antipath"* as one young Odessa Miss called him), a stoop-shouldered, clumsy, unfortunate, fatherless boy in worn boots and tattered student cap with its insignia torn off, had left forever for a life of work, literature, and poetry, for Tyutchev and Walt Whitman.

First he worked putting up posters and as a painter's assistant, later he began to write newspaper articles and translate poetry. He made himself into a man of letters, a writer, and most important, a lifelong, insatiable, active *reader*—not just the "antipath" but the *antipode* of idle, nonreading, ignorant, vulgar, prissy, gambling Odessa. In a letter to a friend he once vindictively characterized *this* Odessa as "a philistine factory." Idleness, in particular intellectual idleness, he considered the epitome of vulgar banality**—so he, the most sociable person on earth, curious about anyone and everyone, able to enliven any group of people with an epigram, a bit of roughhousing with children, or a story of some new literary discovery, hated anything which smacked of idleness: he simply refused to take part in the social rite called "visiting." He went to other people's houses and invited people to his, as one would to a play, a lecture, an exhibition, a debate . . . But going visiting simply to drink tea and gossip (gifts, new shoes, relatives)—he was no good at that. For him our home was primarily a workplace, where he wrestled with some project or other; it's going badly, it's going badly, it's going badly—guests? now? sheer agony!—but finally, it would go well, and then you'd have your celebration. Then there'd be skis, or the sea, or the boat, and children, and a bonfire on the beach, and people. Listeners were needed to find out if the work had really turned out well. And

---

*A game played with special picture cards. (Translator)

**There is no adequate counterpart in English for the Russian word "poshlost," which is used here and throughout the book. The dictionary equivalent "banality" cannot convey the complex and pejorative connotations of the Russian word. (Translator)

off he'd go to Repin's studio to see how the portrait of Korolenko was coming along, or to his neighbors, to Tsensky's or to Korolenko's, to listen to something they'd written and to read his own effort. Now that was a holiday!

The usual, traditional holidays, especially family ones, he couldn't bear—unless he could turn them into a theatrical production, a pointed matching of wits, a general game of some kind. Any silver wedding anniversary sort of occasion seemed to him a total waste of time; a truly work-oriented person just doesn't have time for such empty pursuits.

An entry from his diary is telling.

The year, 1922. Petrograd. Kuokkala is already in the past.

The second birthday of Murochka (Maria), his youngest daughter, my sister. Presents, relatives, friends. All the usual things for a birthday party. Guests.

We read: ". . . it was a joyous day for me, but contaminated by guests. Disgusting. I hate such organized idleness."

If hosts and guests innocently and complacently munching on cake can contaminate a joyous day with their festivities, then what more organized and hateful form of idleness could he imagine than cards?

After all, people play cards to kill time, but a man absorbed in his work has no extra time. For him twenty-four hours a day is not enough; no "philistine factory" for him, no stupid bunch of clerks who've put in their day at work, sat out the required hours, and have nothing to do with their time.

(Go visiting! Play cards by the hour! No, sir!)

Obviously, I only came to understand his thinking and the reasons for his fierce disdain for cards later, when I grew up and came to understand his life story.

I didn't understand the reasons at Kuokkala, but he successfully beat into our heads the certainty that wasting time playing cards was shameful.

One day when we thought he was planning to spend the night in town, he appeared unexpectedly at the door of the veranda and found us playing cards. We weren't playing for money, not even for nuts. We were just playing, playing "war."

He couldn't have been more angry had he found us making counterfeit money. He wasn't even mollified by the fact that we'd made all our own kings and jacks.

Furiously, he ripped the cards from our hands, tore them to pieces, crumpled them and threw the ball as far as he could into the neighbor's field. Then he looked around on the table for something to break, but didn't find anything. Then, striding up and down the veranda, he turned on the main offender—Kolya. Since Kolya was the oldest, he always considered him responsible for everything.

"There's not enough time for English, but there's enough for this abomination. He had fifteen English words to learn, but he . . ."

"Papa, I learned my words," said Kolya. "Test me."

"Learned them! Miscreant! He's found something to boast about! He's doing me a favor! Fifteen words, and not one more! From here to here! And he could learn not fifteen a day, but fifty... His lessons for Vera Mikhailovna aren't done, but he sits here playing cards. And teaching Lida, too. Wretch!"

"Papa, I did my lessons for Vera Mikhailovna," said Kolya.

"So they're done, are they! You could have set yourself some lessons. One more page of history a day, for instance. Some extra math problems... Or what about reading a book; there are a few books around here, for God's sake."

"I just finished *Treasure Island* and I haven't found another yet," said Kolya.

"Imagine that, he needs a breather after *Treasure Island*! So he's doing me a favor by reading. If you didn't feel like reading, why not stoop to something useful... (he improvised feverishly). Like sweeping the porch. Nanny Tonya hasn't sat down all day... And they've been lying around... You could have... (he invented), you could always have carried sand... for cleaning pots... Princelings!"

I'll never forget that evening or the disgusted way he threw the crumpled pack out the window. As if it were a toad. In his eyes cardplaying was the symbol of idleness, the contemptible entertainment of contemptible fools, who valued the pleat in a man's trousers more than his talent and learning.

He went up to his study and slammed the door, but his anger hadn't yet run its course, and he reappeared, leaning over the banister to shout at Kolya:

"Ex-cise-tax collector!" then slammed the door again with all his strength so that the glass rattled on both verandas, upstairs and down.

(Cards weren't all that was forbidden at Kuokkala; wine and tobacco were also against the law. Wine was never served, no matter what the occasion or who the guests; the head of the household didn't smoke, and though guests were permitted to smoke, after a smoker left a kind of disinfection would take place: the butts were hurriedly carried out to the trash pit, the ashtrays washed, and the rooms aired.

At Peredelkino in his last years, he relaxed his custom and allowed wine in the house. Not for himself, but for his guests. But he didn't know how to entertain: he'd get up too quickly and unceremoniously from the table. He was always eager either to get outdoors, to go into the garden with his guests, or to take them to his study—to listen, read, discuss... Sensing that, a guest would drink his glass, grab a quick bite to eat, and stand up. He just never managed to learn the social ritual of sitting around the table in a leisurely fashion.)

Fresh air, poetry, books, contact with lots of different people, improvisations, fairy tales, charades, games with children—those for Kornei Chukovsky were the real source of pleasure and refreshment.

At Kuokkala he not only eagerly played with us in any free time he had, he also carefully guarded our private games and improvisations from outside invasion, even his own—especially those he felt to be the fruit of original inspiration and creativity.

Kolya loved to play make believe. By himself.

"Get out of here," said Kolya to me. "Don't you see I'm dreaming."

This did not at all mean that he sat on a bench, chin in hands, gazing dreamily at the clouds. "Dreaming" in his language meant jumping from stone to stone along the beach right at the water's edge, first hiding from invisible enemies lurking in ambush, then ambushing them himself, or throwing himself into the midst of a crowd of pursuers, smiting them left and right. He jumped tirelessly from stone to stone, waving a stick which served in turn as wheel, boomerang, pike, and sword, all the while quickly and quietly exclaiming:

"They rushed from the deep thicket. Shots rang out, bang, bang, but not a single one grazed his head! His bullets, however, took their toll on his attackers! Crack-crack-crack! sounded from the rock where he lay in wait, rifle to his eye. The dead fell like flies. Horses reared up, throwing their riders from their saddles, and fled in terror back to the prairie."

("Get out of here," he yelled, catching sight of me or Boba. "Can't you see I'm dreaming!")

"Ten bodies lay on the ground. He stood up, straightening to his full height, and gazed across the desert. He knew they'd gather their forces and return. He had no more than three minutes to prepare himself. Help was nowhere to be found. He must strengthen his position."

Throwing aside his stick, Kolya began to crawl frantically along the beach, building up a pile of sand and rocks. I looked on enviously. I wanted to jump from stone to stone, too, and hold a stick up to my eye—crack! crack! But he wouldn't let me play with him. Well, don't take me then, I'll play by myself, but he says I can't even stay on the beach.

No fair!

I ran home to complain. But my complaints had no effect. Our captain, leader, and highest judge, who had so furiously shouted at Kolya just last night about the cards, today didn't want him to be disturbed. He protected his running around on the stones. It was the active working out of imagination and literary recollection in the fresh air. This was Her Royal Highness Play.

He couldn't explain all this to me at the time, but he didn't want to hurt my feelings.

"Lidochek, it's been a long time since I've drawn you a picture," he said in an ingratiating, apologetic voice. "Look, I'll draw you a picture, and you guess what it is."

With pen or pencil he drew wonderfully accurate caricatures. Right away you could guess who was who. In front, the long-nosed baker in his black-brimmed cap, balancing a woven basket on his head, the very one who brought us Vyborg pretzels every Sunday morning. You could almost hear the squeak of his basket. And next, Repin's yardman and coachman, the one who let me braid the mane of Lyuba the horse.

Then Lyuba herself. Her friendly old face.

But today I don't enjoy the pictures. As if I don't understand! He only wants to keep me from bothering Kolya. That's why he's drawing me the yardman and the horse.

But Kolya has taken over the whole beach. All my favorite stones. And it's the same thing almost every day. How many times already have I heard:

"Boba, Lida, don't go that way! Kolya's dreaming over there!"

I don't want pictures. I want justice.

"—And the horses collided as the warriors clashed. And the riders caught each other by the waist with hooks... And Ilya was already flying over his horse's head—to the ground..."

CHAPTER
VI

Our game of games as children was the sea.

Since morning we've been running to the beach to see if we can see Kronstadt. How well can we see it? Is it hiding on the horizon, is it wrapping itself in mist? Kronstadt is our barometer. The thick, dark blue label on the light blue sky and the golden dome of the cathedral, when distinctly visible, are like a navigator's needle pointing to "clear."

Now if only... if only he'll finish his work before dark!

Hanging around near the veranda steps, we listen for sounds from the second floor.

He's coming! He's in a good mood! He's taking the stairs two steps at a time!

In his loud, whistling half-whisper, he's saying:

> Partly for foolish honesty,
> Partly pure simplicity,
> I'll live in lowly poverty,
> And languish in obscurity.[1]

He's in a good mood! Let's go!

He doesn't call to us or acknowledge our presence in any way. Chin held high, he strides down to the beach with a detached, impassive expression, as if he intends to go out on the water alone... But we don't worry, not a bit; the boating ritual has long been worked out to the last detail, and our captain coolly walking past us, head in the air, is all part of the game. He won't go anywhere without us! We fan out, each to his appointed task. We all have our own nautical responsibilities. Boba runs to the shed for the bucket. Kolya and Pavka drag out the heavy oars, two pairs. Ida brings the oarlocks, Matti, the boathook, and I, official "keeper of the fresh water," get a corked bottle of cold water from the icehouse. (Later, in his play *The Potbellied Tsar*, he created for me the role of "Keeper of the Royal Toothpick.")

While waiting for us, he has turned over the wide, heavy fisherman's boat and pushed her into the water. She has no rudder, and the anchor is a stone tied round with a rope. Though heavy, she's roomy. He quickly stows the gear aboard, oarlocks, oars and anchor-stone, and orders us to sit: Kolya or Pavka on the middle seat, the rest, wherever we find ourselves, in the stern, in the bow, or in the bottom. Rolling up his trousers, he pushes the boat off the sand where it settled when we plunked down inside; then tilting her, he climbs aboard himself and standing at his full, enormous height, skillfully steers the boat out to deep water with oar or boathook. Then it's oarlocks into sockets, oars into oarlocks, and we're off! For a minute things don't go right, the oars splash raggedly, he shouts at Kolya, but then the rhythm gets established, and four oars, drops of sunshine dripping from their blades, rise in unison from the water and drop back down again.

The sea is almost flat. Small waves lift the boat gently. The bow makes a wide track. Sea and sky spread out in a vast expanse. The air is so clean, every breath is like a gulp of fresh water. The boat moves easily, calmly, steadily, the water murmuring a little against the side of the boat.

No one feels like talking.

And so we are quiet, watching the shore grow distant.

Silently, we submit to the generous, boundless light, to the gentle rocking motion. The first seagull appears. We can no longer see the rocks on the beach. Now people are no longer visible. The scattered pine trees on the shore merge into a solid, thick, black throng, and indistinguishable behind that swaying throng is our dacha.

The boat moves ahead quickly, obedient to the stroke of the oars. Watching how effortlessly he and Kolya pull on their oars, lifting off their benches a little then settling back down, it seems to me that nothing in the world could be easier than rowing. But once when Kornei Ivanovich, giving into my pleas, sat me next to him and gave me an oar—only one to start with!—I wasn't strong enough to hold, much less to pull it. I wasn't yet six at the time. A few years later, by the time we left Kuokkala forever, I was able to row easily.

Our captain later wrote about how he became familiar with the sea in his reminiscences of Boris Zhitkov.

I will never forget how he began to teach me rowing in the early spring, not in the port, but off Lanzherone, near the deserted beach, in a boat borrowed from a Greek acquaintance.

...His demands knew no bounds. When one of my oars came out of its oarlock, he looked at me with such disgust, I felt like a wretch. He demanded regular, skillful, precise strokes. At first I wielded the heavy oars so feebly and clumsily that more than once he shouted with indignation:

"In front of the shore, you should be ashamed!"

. . . Soon I mastered the oars enough so that Zhitkov decided we could leave the harbor for the open sea, where turbulent, cheerful waves immediately leapt at our tiny craft.

Before I met Zhitkov, I'd never even imagined that such fun existed. Hardly had the first fresh breeze off the Black Sea struck our faces, than I burst at the top of my lungs into the broad, sweeping lines written for just such an occasion:

> Wave, oh how great you are! Wave of the ocean!
> Whose is the feast day you're feasting today?[2]

And here, on the Gulf of Finland, the bright sunshine, smooth stroke of the oars, and expectant children's faces also aroused his thirst for reciting poetry. This thirst was unquenchable in him; from childhood to the last day of his life, poetry was for him an inexhaustible source of delight. He recited poetry often, and always out loud: to himself, privately, in his study; to Repin in his studio or to Repin's guests in the gazebo; to passing students on the beach; to his neighbor friends, Nikolai Fedorovich Annensky, Tatiana Alexandrovna Bogdanovich, and Korolenko; or to us on the way to the post office. And of course out on the water. At sea, he allowed himself free rein. The rhythm of the waves and of the rowing naturally called forth a rhythmic response.

I have never heard poetry recited more beguilingly. It was as if, at these moments, every aspect of his being were concentrated in voice, inflection, lips, and sounds, sounds seeming to cling to lips, and lips to sounds. As a little girl, I first noticed how beautiful his hands were one day when I was listening to him recite poetry out at sea. I've never seen such remarkable hands on anyone since—strong, capable, but unblemished by oar, saw, pail, stone, or shovel, with long fingers which bent back slightly at the tips.

The lyrical side of his nature, usually hidden behind irony, mockery, sarcasm, and passionate disputatiousness, revealed itself more clearly when he recited poetry.

There was a kind of sorcery in his voice when he read great poetry which bewitched both him and us. He often wrote that from childhood on he was accustomed to "get drunk" on poetry. Ecstasy is contagious. We undoubtedly grew drunk listening to him grow drunk on what he was reciting. And all the poetry I ever learned later, on my own, without him, the sound of any sort of poetic line, no matter who recited it, was always connected in my mind to my childhood and his voice.

"Wave, oh how great you are! Wave of the ocean!" he began, thrusting forward on his oars and rocking a little. "Whose is the feast day you're feasting today?"

> Billows roll on, in loud sparkling commotion,
> All-seeing stars calmly gaze down our way, . . .[3]

he recites in a loud, singsong, passionate, almost prayerful voice, and it seems to me the boat no longer obeys wave and oar, but like oar, wave, and everything else has become thrall to his voice.

When he recited poetry for us on our seagoing excursions, was he engaged in that poetic education he wrote so much about later and whose lack he so bitterly lamented? Yes and no. No, because he had not yet developed the techniques and methods for poetic education which he set forth in detail in articles written after the revolution; at that point he had only taken note of the match between poetry and children, between poetry and different ages, of the stages of perception. No, his actions weren't yet conscious or by design; if he'd been out in the boat alone, without an audience, he would probably have recited the same verses he recited for us. Yet, he was certainly engaged in our poetic education! The effort was not perhaps a formal and deliberate attempt to educate: he was—how should I put it?—making us fall in love with poetry. In his books he asserts that the teacher of literature's first job is to make children fall in love with poetry. On our seagoing excursions he inspired that love in us.

Certainly, he also understood that a child's ear for rhythm is much keener than an adult's can ever be. If by reciting us enormous amounts of poetry he was taking only the first, most elementary step in poetic pedagogy, it was the one without which *any* further step is impossible; he charmed us with poetry, enthralled us with it, as some children are enthralled by music.

(He already understood that giving a listener any kind of information about poetry—historical or structural—*before poetry itself* has become a vital part of his life is useless, academic, even harmful. Why cram the heads of adults and children with facts about the rhythmical structure of *The Bronze Horseman*, the obstacles to its first publication, and the way critics received it when at last it appeared, if the listeners have not experienced the joy of reciting it out loud to themselves upon waking up and going to sleep:

> For now Nevá, her flow arrested
> By the relentless sea-wind's force,
> Reared up in fury, backward-crested,
> And drowned the islands in her course.)[4]

" . . . I belong to that group of eccentrics who love poetry more than any other art form," wrote Kornei Ivanovich in his book *From Two to Five*, "and who know from experience the incomparable pleasure poetry gives to those who can appreciate it."

30

Commenting on those untalented teachers who through clumsy ignorance destroy children's feeling for the rhythm of poetry and thus deprive them of the legacy of the great poets, he continued: "Is it possible that not one of them [the new generation of children] is to be granted the extraordinary joy of reading, for example, *The Bronze Horseman*, of delighting in each rhythmic beat, each pause, each pyrrhic foot? Is it possible that this great happiness, from which we have derived so much delight, is to be denied them? Do we have the right to keep this happiness selfishly for ourselves, not sharing it with anyone else? Are we not obliged to pass it on to our children?"[5]

Happiness, happiness... He did not keep this happiness selfishly for himself. During our boating expeditions at Kuokkala, he shared these joys munificently with us.

> Galloping waves of the Mediterranean
> Dangerously fondle our ship, unrestraining.
> Staunchly the captain moves up to the bow
> Shrill sounds his whistle. And joining the engine
> Our big, white sail billows out with a vengeance.
> Foaming and sighing, the sea runs below.
> Onward. The wheels of the powerful engine
> Plow through the high-crested waves, unrelenting,
> Wind fills the sails and the shore seems to flee.
> We are alone with the waves and the ocean,
> Only a seagull follows our motion,
> Soaring, white-winged, 'twixt the sky and the sea.
> . . . .
> . . . .
> Many the country I've left far behind me,
> Much have I borne, I have suffered wildly,
> With troubling questions I've managed to cope,
> Felt spurious joys or known actual failures
> Ere the strong hands of Marseillian-born sailors
> Lifted our anchor, the symbol of hope.
> . . . .
> Far or in reach of the shore, need I measure?
> Not if the heart brings to shore such a treasure.
> I see Fetida; my fate at my birth
> Gleaned from the azure-blue urn by her powers.
> Soon I shall see old Livorno, its towers,
> Soon I shall see that Elysium on earth.[6]

What a lot of unfamiliar words and names! Fetida, glean, Elysium, Livorno! But he didn't explain a thing, not a single word, only solemnly

31

announced, "Baratynsky." Together with him we gave ourselves up to the energy of the rhythm, no less powerful in these lines than the energy of the wind.

"Wind fills the sails, and the shore seems to flee."

If one of us—I, at six, or Kolya, at nine—had tried to read these verses, we would have stumbled over the first Fetida and set the book aside. But he recited them to us. And from his recitation, even though he didn't explain anything, we understood not just the beauty of the verses as a great work of art, the beauty of their sound and rhythmic pattern, but also the general idea, that which one might broadly call the content. Not the meaning of each separate word and line, but that which *was contained* in the fantastical way they were woven into lines and stanzas and fused together by the force of the rhythm.

Rhythm is the best interpreter of meaning. And this interpreter, clearly highlighted by the voice of the reciter, told us that these lines were about the free will of a man joyfully crossing the ocean, about the happy, triumphant freedom of breasting the stormy waves, and about the fact that this man will soon see a place more wonderful than any other, called by the marvelous and mysterious name, Elysium.

> Soon I shall see old Livorno, its towers,
> Soon I shall see that Elysium on earth.

Where's Livorno? What's Elysium mean? I don't know. There's something golden in all those "z's": azure, Elysium, on earth.* Yes, I do know: the "Elysium on earth" is something blissful made out of pure gold, to which he has been aspiring—and he has now reached it.

> . . . We are alone with the waves and the ocean,
> Only a seagull follows our motion,
> Soaring, white-winged, 'twixt the sky and the sea.

How many times had I seen and heard seagulls! But the amazing height to which the word "white-winged" was lifted in Baratynsky's poem, reinforced by a rhythmic lifting in the voice as it pronouced the line, with a tiny pause after that word—"Soaring white-winged (pause), 'twixt the sky and the sea"—made me experience for the first time the great space between sea and sky, and a seagull at play in this expanse.

I am six years old. In two years I will go to the gymnasium, and there, in time, I will learn in geography class where Livorno is, and in history class what Elysium means. Or maybe some winter evening, he will open the *En-*

---

*In Russian, all these words, including "golden," contain or begin with a "z." (Translator) *cyclopedia Britannica* and himself show us the map of Italy and the Mediterranean Sea. But now, from his voice and these lines of poetry, I learn something it's impossible to learn from either a geography book or an encyclopedia—the power of the waves, the power of will, the vastness of the earth, the allure of travel to foreign lands. *This* knowledge one can gain only from works of art—short of taking the same trip across the Mediterranean Sea. Even then, by the way, you won't learn that "the towers of Livorno" are not just the towers of a certain Italian town, but the fulfillment of a dream.

In my time I've heard a great many poetry readings. I've listened to actors and poets alike. I've heard Yakhontov, Anton Schwartz, Kachalov, Zhuravlev. Each one of them performed in his own distinctive manner. I've heard poets—Mayakovsky, Blok, Akhmatova, Tsvetaeva, Kuzmin, Mandelstam, Gumilyov, Khodasevich, Pasternak, Klyuev, Esenin, Zabolotsky, Tvardovsky, Berggolts, Marshak, Petrovykh, Vvedensky, Kharms, Kvitko, Kornilov, Samoyilov, Mezhirov, Iosif Brodsky, Kushner, Slutsky. Each of them, too, of course, recited in his own way. The now conversational, now emotional intonation of Mayakovsky in no way resembled the latent passion concealed by outward restraint of Blok's recitation (his mournful, muffled voice seemed simply to list the words); I heard the candid, wide open recitation of Pasternak, so completely unlike the severe, serious, reserved recitation of Akhmatova (she remained closed, even as she opened herself)—yet different as they were, the poets' recitations all had something indefinable in common which contrasted with the actors' recitations. Poets do not take license with their poetry, although as creators they, presumably, have the right to do whatever they choose; they recite obeying the invisible music embedded in every line, the poem's rhythmical movement, which, in harmony with the flow of thought and feeling and the reciter's breath, creates the majesty, the omnipotence of poetry. Actors take license; one tries to create the "mood," another to play the role of the hero, a third, that of the author, in general they try to illustrate the poetry, to enrich it, by gesture or voice, not trusting the power of the poetry itself.

(I will never forget how Kachalov, reading Blok's lines:

> Then came the hour: you left the house forever.
> I threw the cherished ring into the night.[7]

gestured with his arm as though he were throwing the cherished ring out the window, and reciting from "The Scythians" the line "breaking the horses' broad backs" pretended to be breaking a stick.

The words and rhythm didn't seem expressive enough to him. He thought he'd help them out.)

Kornei Ivanovich recited poetry like a poet, not an actor. He tried not to add anything of his own to the intonation or rhythm as he recited, instead his voice, his whole being obeyed the rhythmic movement, which made clear the meaning of even the most complicated verse, even to very young children. That's why his recitations made comprehensible to us poems which used many words we didn't know or depicted events which were beyond our experience.

On these seagoing excursions, these excursions into poetry, he almost never explained a word to us. He would announce only the name of the poet, hoping that we would learn to recognize the uniqueness of the intonation and never confuse it with any other, as easily as children learn to distinguish a spruce tree from a pine, an aspen from a birch. This is Baratynsky. "Wind fills the sails, and the shore seems to flee." Do you hear it? And this is Nekrasov. "Sorrowful sorrow embraces the world."[8] Unthinkable to mistake the one for the other.

He often played the game of reciting us some lines from a poem we didn't know and asking us to guess who the author might be; and when my brother was ten and I, seven, he explained the basic metrical patterns to us, showing us how to indicate them, and then created the game of seeing who could more quickly determine the meter. Later on, he began to tell us the life stories of different poets, Shevchenko or Byron, Pushkin or Lermontov. Still later, to demonstrate the relationship between rhythm and meter.

But all that came afterwards.

At Kuokkala, in the boat, his goal was not to increase our knowledge, but our joy.

And this joy allowed us unsuspectingly, little by little to get to know the world. And Russia.

We lived in Finland* all year round. The only part of Russia I knew at that time was Suvorovsky Prospect in Petersburg and the Tavrichesky Garden, where we were taken to play when I was very small. As to the real Russia, I was thirteen before I spent time in a little village outside Porkhov. I saw Moscow for the first time when I was sixteen, and Russia's vast countryside as it flew past the windows of my train on the way to the Crimea when I was seventeen. But by the time I was six or seven, I already had learned something important about Russia from the rhythms of Nekrasov, conveyed through Kornei Chukovsky's reciting of his poetry.

About its downtrodden peasant huts. About their defenselessness. About parting. About meeting. About death.

> Like living steppe, rye fields extending,
> No mountain peak, no sea, no manse...
> I thank you, native land unending,
> For your restorative expanse![9]

---

*Finland was a part of the Russian Empire until the revolution. (Translator)

Here, even the "I thank you" sounds like a groan, and the expanse not only restores, it also injures, and the native land unending sounds like sobbing.* This was my first sense of Russia, which I received as a gift from Nekrasov.

And then there was *Red-nose Frost!*

> Cruelly the blizzard wind wailing
> Lashed at the windows with snow.
> The sun rose reluctant and paling,
> Slowly that morning unveiling,
> A sorrowful portrait below.

The thrice-repeated rhyme in his recitation was like a triple spasm of pain. "Wailing," and "paling," were exhausting enough, and the voice grew exhausted, the addition of the third "unveiling" was almost too much to bear:

> Cruelly the blizzard wind wailing
> Lashed at the windows with snow.
> The sun rose reluctant and paling,
> Slowly that morning unveiling,
> A sorrowful portrait below.
> Savraska, in harness, head bobbing,
> Stands at the gate with the sled.
> With no extra words, with no sobbing,
> The villagers bring forth the dead.
> "Now, gee up, Savrasushka! Gee up!
> Give all you've got to the yoke!
> You pulled long and hard for your master,
> Pull one last time!" cry the folk...

With no sobbing? The very lines are sobs. Sobbing for the defenselessness of the land. For the futility of toil. The sobs are no less clear in these lines than in those where it is openly described:

> September din—my much beloved country,
> Sodden with rain, was sobbing with each breath.
> A flock of birds was flying black above me
> As if they sensed the cold approach of death.[10]

---

*The word "native"—*rodnaya*—sounds quite similar to the word "sobbing"— *rydanye*. (Translator)

...Kolya and Pavka took turns at the oars when they grew tired, but he continued without a break to row and recite. He recited for us Pushkin, Polonsky, Fet, Lermontov.

I remember the unusual way I first heard the sound of Fet's poetry: not on its own, but incorporated into a poem of Polonsky's. Polonsky wrote a poem for Fet's fiftieth birthday in which the first lines of the first verse are a sort of concentrate of his friend's poetry, written not in his, Polonsky's, style, but in Fet's.

> The nights went on—stars a-twinkling in the blackness
> their rays of light were scattering...
> Tears streaming downwards—all sobbing was love; then upsprang
> Dawn, warm and red, and the daydreams we were secretly
> in our hearts fostering
> Trill of the nightingale banished—and loudly soon rang
> Wave of the storm-angry sea—ideas ripened, and—hovering
> Gray wingéd seagulls...
> This game all the gods were engendering;
> In this their world-spanning game Fet quickly joined and sang...[11]

(The way Polonsky speaks about poetry and the poet in these lines is somewhat similar to what Blok said later in a speech about Pushkin: he spoke of poetry not just as a phenomenon of culture—but of nature and the elements as well.

The comparison between Polonsky's idea and Blok's certainly didn't occur to me in Kuokkala, but later in Petrograd, in 1921, when I heard Blok give a lecture on Pushkin at the "House of the Literati." What sort of comparison could I have made at age six or seven! However, as a child, out on the water, the voice, the cries of the gulls, the waves and the words—nature and poetry—were fused together by the moment itself. And I imagined that Fet was a kind of bird, perhaps also a seagull, only one that sang.)

The first verse, where Polonsky was Fet—which we, of course, didn't understand at the time—Kornei Ivanovich recited without taking a breath, quickly, faster and faster, as if trying with his voice to fly up as fast as possible, so as to dart down from there, from this height, onto the last two slow, steady lines, for the sake of which all the rest had been written.

Faster, faster, up, up—almost like a tongue twister and without taking a breath:

> ...and the daydreams we were secretly in our hearts fostering
> Trill of the nightingale banished—and loudly soon rang
> Wave of the storm-angry sea—ideas ripened, and—hovering
> Gray wingéd seagulls...

Pause. Slowly. Almost syllable-by-syllable. He drew out the word "gods," as if it had at least three "o's," in the "world-spanning game" he emphasized the "r," and he pronounced the name Fet firmly, steadily:

> This game all the go-o-ods were engendering;
> In this their world-spanning game
>> Fet
> quickly joined and sang. . .

Probably to insure that we heard the sounds of this mysterious bird, Fet, competing with the gods and the storms in his song, he recited us next his favorite, tree-rocking Fet dactyls:

> The spruce with its branches the path it kept hid from me.
>> Wind blows. Alone in the wood
> Noisy, and scary, and gloomy, and happy we. . .
>> Can't understand it at all.[12]

. . . When we returned to our senses from Fet, we usually found ourselves so far out to sea that the shore was barely visible. Time for a swim.

(Not Boba and me—we didn't know how to swim yet and bathed only off the beach, out here we were the guardians of the trousers, shirts, oars. Nothing else.)

The seafarers, baked by the sun, began to strip off their shirts as if they thought the sea might dry up or run out of water before they could get their clothes off. They dove eagerly into the water—hairy and enormous, he was first of all. At first he would swim around the boat, not too far away, splashing Boba and me and the poor shirts and trousers with quantities of cold spray. Then he would swim far off. Then he would stroke back and, counting out loud to himself, "one, two, three!"—disappear right before our eyes.

This was the major moment of the swim. And though I never admitted it, the most excruciating, terrifying moment of my childhood.

He's not there anymore. I look at the place where his head dropped out of sight and whisper to myself: "Come up, come up, come up." I can't understand how Boba can play with his bucket at this moment, or Kolya and Pavka laugh and hit each other on the back. He's not there anymore. He has dived down in front of our eyes and disappeared lots of times before and always returned. But what if this time he doesn't reappear—ever? Just a minute ago his eyes, his hands, his legs, his voice, his hair were here—and—maybe never again. Only his shirt is still here. I look and look. Come up, come up, come up! And there finally—his head. It never appears in the place where it disappeared and which I've been watching with all my might, but far, far away in a different, unexpected spot, shoulders and head, his hair all smoothed down by the water, head somehow streaming as water pours off it in rivulets. A mighty spluttering. He must have gone at least ten papas deep. His long fingers cover, then clear off his face. He spits. He has turned blue. Grabbing hold of the side of the boat with blue fingers, tipping it so Boba and I nearly somersault into the water, he throws one leg after the other inside, shivering all over, pulls on his trousers and shirt, then orders Kolya and Pavka to return without delay.

I'm saved. He's here.

Once he has warmed himself up rowing, he begins to recite poetry again, this time happy, light-hearted, nonsensical, sprightly verses.

> The candles bright, the candles light,
> Do burn, my lords, do burn.
> But did they see, or did they not—
> That you'll never learn.[13]

Or:

> Like an apple pink
> And always most untidy,
> It isn't that he drinks—
> He's just happy every Friday.
> With money—he will play,
> With none—he'll do without it,
> Laughs all the more about it!
> "So what!"—he'll calmly say,
> "So what!"—he'll calmly say,
> "Who cares what comes hereafter!
> Ay-ay, I'll die...
> Ay-ay, I'll die...
> Ay-ay, I'll die of laughter!"[14]

Or:

> By strange and ancient custom,
> I criticized ballet.
> But then field glasses proffered
> A general one day.
> . . . .
> Don't read that book of Buckle's, Sir!
> He's not so good, that Buckle,
> As a fine set of binoculars...
> Go get yourself a couple![15]

How we loved this treat—the happy rhyme, "binoculars—Buckle's, Sir"! (Obviously, there was no knowing anything about Buckle.*) We doubled over, collapsing with laughter. We repeated: "Go get yourself a couple!" stressing the "g" sounds.

He'd have already started something new:

> Underneath our tsar's hand,
> The system's so political,
> Though there's no Timashev
> The flogging's still terrifical.
> Near Tsepnoy Bridge, that building,
> Whatever is it for?
> Comes out proclamation—
> They whip you 'til you're sore.[16]

Who was Timashev? What bridge? What building? Which Tsar? At the moment he explained nothing. Explain, explain, he'll explain everything when the time comes. He apparently agreed completely with Tolstoy that children before the age of ten don't have a sense of history, so why explain; but a child's ear for rhythm and his sense of humor is heightened, so he used these attributes to give us a sense of the satirical as well as the lyrical.

"The candles light, the candles bright" we turned into a counting rhyme. "Standing in a circle—who will go first? The-candles-light-the-candles-bright-do-burn-my-lords-do-burn." "Tsepnoy Bridge"—into a taunt. We understood the main idea in these lines: that someone brave and daring is mocking someone powerful and cowardly.

> Comes out proclamation—
> They whip you 'til you're sore!

We also loved Pushkin's similarly merry "Delibash."

> Bullets fly behind the hillocks;
> Camps opposing, set to clash;
> On the hill before our cossacks
> Circles a red delibash.

Pushkin warns the cossack against the delibash and the delibash against the cossack, but in vain.

---

*Henry Thomas Buckle, a nineteenth-century English historian. (Translator)

> Riding, shouting, now they strike...
> Look at them! How spirited...
> The delibash is on a pike,
> And the cossack's lost his head.

Rhythm is the best interpreter of meaning. Although the lines describe war and double murder, the rhythm speaks of play. Not for nothing did Pushkin in another four-line stanza call a bloody skirmish "a lively game." These lines don't in the least inspire terror, to the contrary, they inspire fun. And responding to the truth of the rhythm, upon any success—jumping off the fence, turning over a heavy stone, driving off a wasp, breaking off an icicle—we would shout:

> Look at them! How spirited...
> The delibash is on a pike,
> And the cossack's lost his head.

CHAPTER
VII

By no means all our nautical expeditions turned out so idyllically.

Anyone who lives on the coast of the Gulf of Finland only in summer, in June, in July, doesn't really know it. The gulf in summer pretends, à la Pasternak, to be toylike, made for children:

> You are visiting with children,

says Pasternak of the Black Sea, not the Gulf of Finland—

> But with what an unimaginable storm
> Do you respond,
> When the deep distance calls you home![1]

Inevitably every fall, in this not-as-it-appears, apparently made-for-children Gulf of Finland, both inexperienced dachniks and very experienced fishermen perish. I first saw a bloated dead body washed up on the shore on a patch of rotting reeds when I was seven years old. I couldn't believe it was a human being. I watched them cover him with matting... The Gulf of Finland is a difficult, treacherous bay; during the summer, when it reminds one of warm broth poured by mistake into a shallow bowl instead of a deep one, it harbors great dangers, shoals and rocks near the shore and fickle winds, and in the fall, powerful storms and squalls.

Nearly every week during the fall, the deep distance of the Baltic Sea calls to its gulf, and the gulf responds to every call with a storm which tears up great pines by the roots and throws them on the ground; a storm which drives the Neva River backwards and floods the harbor, islands, and sometimes even the major streets of Petersburg; and during our time in Kuokkala, would scatter the baskets full of rocks and sand, over which we had labored so hard, as casually and easily as if they had been empty matchboxes.

It was terrifying to be wakened in the night by the crash of the waves and the howl of the wind, which seemed to be testing if the roof would hold. It was even more terrifying to go out on the porch in the morning and see traces of foam and bits of seaweed hanging on bushes and stumps—during the night, waves had come all the way up there!—to see a monstrous hole, a grave really, in which water was slowly but surely accumulating, and over which exposed tree roots bristled like thick spider legs. And the fallen spruces! One was lying on the ground, another, broken, was tipping over, half-lying across others which had survived intact. We'd been lucky; the tree had not crashed down on the roof. And since it had fallen at night, no one had been anywhere nearby.

Kornei Ivanovich loved to describe himself as a frivolous person. In fact, throughout his life carelessness was as characteristic of him as stubbornness and strength of will. And a kind of childish belief in happy endings to bad situations.

One young poetess, who had never seem him with children, wrote him in 1912 that he was probably a very "tender" and "childlike" father.

She was right.

One day we nearly died thanks to his careless childlikeness. He decided to set out on the water one murky, windy, doubtful day in early fall with five little children in the boat, small, smaller and smallest, his own and others, not bothering to wait for the third rower, Kolya's friend, Pavka.

He had finished some article or some part of an article which had given him a lot of trouble. He had to celebrate! (But he didn't look at the horizon.)

When we were already a good distance from the shore, the sky grew dark and the wind came up. It is three in the afternoon, but the sea and the sky are shrouded in darkness. Only the waves show white. Kronstadt has disappeared as if it never existed, the shore also. The seagulls fly up then drop, crying more and more harshly. Then—the storm; the first lightning in the black sky, the first thunder, most terrible of all, torrents of rain. The overloaded boat is already low in the water; as the pouring rain sluices into it from the heavens, it sits lower and lower. Kolya and the captain row desperately for the shore, but the wind is blowing offshore and our little craft hardly moves. We are wet through and through, chilled to the bone, and for the first time in my life I hear how sharply and distinctly teeth chatter. My own and other people's.

We are shivering all over. Even in winter it's not as cold as this. The wind and rain are crueller than the frost.

I bail water with the pail, the littler ones—Boba and an even younger child!—with their hands. But how are we to compete with the driving rain?

The boat rides ever lower. The waves are on the verge of pouring over the side.

The wind has torn one of the oars out of Kolya's hand. Kolya bends to grab it and drops the oarlock.

He starts to cry.

Now our captain is our sole rower and our sole hope.

I don't know if he would have survived that day if he hadn't had children with him. I think his sense of guilt about us made him fearless and strong. And grown up. Before our very eyes he was transformed into the all-powerful giant he seemed in our games.

What then he only seemed, he now became.

He who never sang, suddenly began to sing, or more accurately, to yell, outshouting the wind with a tremendous voice. He commanded us to join him. Not once did he scold Kolya. He rowed, puffing out his chest in show, just as he did when someone tossed the stick back at him. He acted as though he were thoroughly enjoying himself. He took off his jacket, as if he were suffering from the heat, and tossed it at the heads of Boba, Matti and me, who were clinging together on one seat.

"Splendid!" he cried. "Now you look like a broody-hen with her chicks. 'Ay-ay, I'll die, ay-ay, I'll die, ay-ay, I'll die of laughter!'"

After half an hour we caught sight of the shore. Not our part of the shore, someone else's, unfamiliar, unknown, but the shore. However, there was no way to put in there. The wind was driving the boat back out to sea. It seemed our captain and rower wielded his oars in vain: we were making no headway.

But it only seemed that way.

The shore, black in the darkness, was drawing closer.

A little cottage had become visible. Perhaps it was small, perhaps a little lopsided. Yet immediately the black sky, white waves, lightning and pouring rain lost their unassailable menace.

A cottage! Human habitation! Warmth.

False joy. As if we couldn't perish within sight of the shore! The hardest part lay ahead—landing.

Our captain, in trousers and shirt, jumped overboard when the water was up to his shoulders. Only his head poked above the waves. He pulled the boat to shore, in danger every second of stepping into some unseen hole or smashing the boat on a rock. Waves splashed over his head.

Closer to shore, once it got shallower and less dangerous, he told Kolya to jump out of the boat. Together they dragged the boat even closer. Somehow or other the captain secured the boat with the anchor-stone and carried us to shore one by one, shouting to each one:

"Run! Run! Don't stand still! Run around!"

Then he dragged the boat ashore and made for the cottage. We followed right behind him.

An old Finnish woman, without a word, began to pull apart her big bed. In a minute all five of us, rubbed down, dry, and wrapped in old but clean rags, lay like a row of logs across the bed under a heavy blanket.

Our captain pointed a questioning finger at a cloth rug. The old woman nodded. He gathered up the rug in his arms, went out into the entrance way, and returned looking like a scaly snake, naked but wrapped from head to toe in rough matting.

Even the warm, dry bed was not enough to take off the chill. It took two full samovars of hot tea to warm us up again.

At last our teeth stopped chattering, our clothes dried out, and we returned to Kuokkala by train, leaving the boat with the old woman.

We walked up to our house. The door was locked. No one was there. Not a light in a window.

No one answered our knock.

Not Mama, not Nanny Tonya.

We ran to the beach. The rain had let up, the thunder and lightning had long ago ended, but the waves raged on. There on the beach, clinging together in the complete darkness, stood a group of women. The mothers of the other children, our mama, and our nanny Tonya. They were looking at the crashing waves. And they were weeping. Some silently, some with sobs and lamentations.

That was the kind of trouble our childlike father got into!

These women, clinging together on the beach and weeping in the darkness, our mother weeping—that was much more terrible than the storm we had just been through.

"The children are home," said our captain. He said it in a quiet, doleful, beaten way, totally different from the victorious way one usually announces good news, or he himself, three hours earlier, had shouted in the face of danger:

> Ay-ay, I'll die...
> Ay-ay, I'll die...
> Ay-ay, I'll die of laughter.

He sounded dejected, wretched, guilty.

Probably, only at that moment, did he understand what he had done.

He'd nearly drowned us. Not only that. Perhaps someone would come down with pneumonia. And worst of all, the moment we made it to shore, he should have, absolutely ought to have, left us in the care of the old woman and come directly home so as not to add a single moment to the mothers' anguish.

But he didn't remain repentant for long. He wasn't given to extended grief.

The next day at lunch, when Kolya and I began competing with each other to describe the details of the previous day's adventures:

"Enough! Enough!" he shouted. (He couldn't stand dwelling on unpleasant things.) "You got soaked, good and soaked... Are you going to waste a lot of time talking about such trifles? You're alive? You're healthy? Now be happy!"

44

CHAPTER

VIII

Once, during a conversation about bashfulness, a friend of my parents who'd just returned to Petersburg from Moscow was imprudent enough to admit that she'd been too shy to become acquainted with any of the other passengers in her four-person compartment. She had said only two things the entire time: "Thank you!" (when someone had helped her with her suitcase) and "good-bye" as she got off the train.

Kornei Ivanovich flew into a mock rage upon hearing this story: "How untalented of you! If I'd been in your place, I'd have learned their life stories...Once upon a time in Odessa there lived a young jeweler's daughter, who said: 'I never say hello to strangers.' As for me, I would have been disappointed in myself if I hadn't become acquainted with everybody in the train, not just the people in my compartment and my car, but all the passengers, no matter how many, and the engineer, fireman and conductors to boot. I'm restless, flighty, chatty, and curious."

And truly, in the rare minutes, hours or days when he wasn't swamped with work, people fascinated him. He looked on every new acquaintance as a treat. Another, another, and still another. New, unknown... Once, during his Peredelkino years, I said to him: "How can you stand the eternal crush? So many strangers every day?"

He answered: "So many? To my mind, there are few. When I'm not working, I'd like a new person to appear on my doorstep every minute."

His answer was both artless and accurate. If a guest appeared at the wrong time, distracting him from his work, Kornei Ivanovich got angry at us for not protecting him well enough. Sometimes he'd even hide. But the dream of a new person a minute was at the same time sincere. The moment he put down his pen or book, he thirsted for contact with people, particularly new people. An adult or child he'd never met or did not yet fully know was always enticing to him. Us, his own children, he loved, devoting to us care, attention and energy; however, other people had a definite, if temporary, advantage over us—their novelty. He knew us by heart:

The unknown I somehow prefer to
All those whom I already know.[1]

He wanted to inspect every new person inside and out; to inspect him, set him in motion, or more precisely, take him apart as children want to take apart a new toy: what sort of spring makes the bear growl or the soldier salute?

In his much later years, when he rode in his own car from Peredelkino to Moscow, he always picked up anyone thumbing a ride and also offered rides to people walking at the side of the road—seeing an old man with a sack on his back or a woman with a child in her arms, he'd rattle the door and say, "Get in, I'll give you a lift!" He'd pick them up out of a sincere wish to help the encumbered pedestrian, combined with his innate curiosity. He simply couldn't drive *past* anyone.

What sort of springs propelled this new, hiterto unknown person? What did he do? What motivated him, what made him happy and unhappy?

Neither the travels of his youth nor the slow rambles around Peredelkino in his later years were ever uneventful. His diary includes many noteworthy descriptions of chance encounters.

He is walking down the road. Women are paving the roadway. Near them, some children. Why are women doing such heavy work, not machines or men? Why is there no nursery school? Today he strolled with a middle-aged woman, formerly a schoolteacher, now a writer, author of several books. Turned out she didn't know Zhukovsky. Not "The Goblet" or "The Cranes of Ibycus." How can she call herself a teacher? A writer, even an intelligent person? "How lazy! How boring!" said he angrily. "An ignorant, unedu-cated watchman interests me. I can learn something from him: he has many skills and knows many things I don't. We have something to talk about. But a writer who doesn't know literature—now that's nonsense, a sham, a fabrication."

Sometimes he would return from a walk truly delighted. Here's his entry for 13 October 1953.

"A Bashkir came up to me, a bareheaded student; we struck up a conver-sation. Strong white teeth, a pleasant smile. Purity of soul, nobility, intel-lectual curiosity. He knows Pushkin, translates Lermontov into Bashkir. Direct, calm, thoughtful—he comforted me a great deal—and was some-how in harmony with the fine, sunny day. He's studying at the literature in-stitute, attends Bondi's lectures. For some reason I consider the meeting with him a special event."

When I observed Kornei Ivanovich's life in Peredelkino, it sometimes seemed to me that the "Writers' Retreat," built in the late fifties on the same street as his dacha, was built at the behest of some kind fate pur-posely for him. Here were people, life stories—not the neighbors he already knew by heart, but constantly new and changing ones... In his free time, he went to the "Writers' Retreat" almost every day, combining his walk with meeting people: sometimes friends, but more often, people he didn't know, or a combination of both, or anybody at all—in the hallway, in the dining room. Those who wanted to would walk him home, and on the way he'd get to know them all as a group and each one individually, and invite them to visit him. Thus he satisfied his need for contact with people, especially new, unexplored people.

(He had the same craving for letters. After all, letters are also people. You arrive in Peredelkino, bearing a bundle of letters addressed to him at his Moscow address. The bundle lies quietly on the desk. But he can't finish his conversation: the letters exert such a strong attraction. It's not that he's expecting a specific letter from a specific person. No. He was always looking forward to hearing from someone he didn't know. Perhaps a word about *From Two to Five*? or *Alive as Life*? Perhaps someone has been inspired by his love for the writer whose soul he revered above all others? whose path, both in literature and life, whose relationships with people, he devotedly understood and secretly tried to imitate? Perhaps he has imbued someone with his love for Chekhov?

As he spoke, Kornei Ivanovich would be looking greedily at the letters. Finally, he'd grab the scissors. His long fingers hovering over the bundle, he'd make his choice like a child choosing from a box of candy, saying as he did so: "And the go-o-ods don't know—which one he'll choose!"[2]

Then with the scissors he'd attack some envelope or other written in an unfamiliar hand... Perhaps, miracle of miracles, there might be some poetry? Not hackwork, which people sent him by the pound, but the real thing?)

But all that was later, in his old age and my adulthood. I return to my childhood, to his youth. In Kuokkala when I was a child, he always took us with him to see how a house was built, a road repaired, a well dug, a railroad track laid down. Technology didn't interest him, but he admired intensely the human genius it represented. He didn't understand anything technical, but he never ceased to marvel at the telegraph, and later at the flight to the moon. From his childhood until his eighty-seventh year, people were his primary interest. Who was a craftsman, a master, who, a mediocre tinkerer? Mastery—of any kind—he respected enormously. And he loved to listen to lively, vigorous language.

Intrigued as he was by all kinds of work and all kinds of people, the phenomenon that interested him most was the creation of art, and the person who interested him most was the creator of art, the artist. The human being who created works of artistic value—especially literary works.

(Didn't all Kornei Chukovsky's critical work arise from a desire to get inside a piece of art by examining its external aspects, its style—to "take it apart" in order to understand the individuality of its creator?)

Artistic work. The brush, the pencil, the pen. Particularly the pen. The human being creating literature. Talent.

No other interest of his could compare with this one. This reverence, this religion was the air we breathed from our earliest youth.

In 1905, as a young man, he wrote his wife: "Art acts upon me so powerfully, I am ready to kiss the hands of the artist."

In 1908 he wrote an article entitled "Tolstoy as an Artistic Genius." Reissuing the article fifty years later, he described it in his introduction as a "youthful hymn" to Tolstoy.

Like all Kornei Chukovsky's articles, it was an analysis, but at the same time, in its own way, it was a sort of "hymn."

It concluded with these words: "...suddenly you are overcome by the thought...that nowhere, nowhere else...in the world could such a person arise, and...you are moved to tears, and feel that there could be no greater happiness than to press this old hand which has made us happy, justified us, blessed us...and cover it with grateful tears."

That could have come from the letter written five years earlier: "...I feel ready to kiss the hands of the artist."

Art stood at the center of his spiritual world for more than six decades. Man—the artist. The unique, singular talent which is unlike any other.

In his last article, published posthumously,[3] he called himself the "humbly enthusiastic listener" of the great lyric poets of the beginning of the century. Definitely "humble," because he never admitted to any talent of his own. (Note these citations from his letters and diaries of different periods: "What kind of writer am I? An unskilled laborer, a feuilletonist, a journalist." "I have never considered myself talented..." "I don't have a high opinion of my own writing, but I am literate and hardworking.") And certainly "enthusiastic": for him a person of talent was crowned with a sort of halo (not always, to his amazement, visible to others); the talented person was lit with a kind of sun whose rays hid human failings from his usually sharp and mocking eyes, especially in the first flush of admiration.

However, Kornei Chukovsky found more than one way to celebrate the delight he felt in the presence of creative talent.

He "got drunk on poetry," but he also parodied the verse of Pushkin, Nekrasov, and Lermontov and enjoyed other people's parodies of Lermontov, Nekrasov, Mayakovsky, and Blok.

His criticial articles were rarely "hymns." He had a reputation, instead, for pointed, combative, impassioned criticism. His critical works were always critiques, analyses; sharp, unexpected, and fresh, they made the reader look again at an apparently familiar author (his articles on Leonid Andreev, Korolenko, Bryusov, Bunin, Blok were of this type); sometimes his critiques led to utter annihilation, outright murder ("Third Rate," his articles on Charskaya, Artsybashev, Verbitskaya). That irrepressible love for art, that dream of covering the hand of Lev Tolstoy with grateful tears, could

48

turn to hatred—a keen hatred for the routine, vulgar, false, and imitative—for work he deemed careless, mercenary, mechanical and indifferent.

"Why is it that the rape of an eight-year-old girl is illegal and punishable with hard labor," he asked in a letter to a friend, "while the rape of Tyutchev or Baratynsky is not only permitted but profitable?

"Take the selected works of the Russian poets edited by Salnikov, Bonch-Bruyevich, P. Ya. et al.—what are they but the rape of all the Russian poets, individually and at once. But these villains are not hung, no, their works are printed and sold in great numbers."

Such were the "hymns" his reverence for Baratynsky and Tyutchev sometimes gave rise to. Why not sentence the perverters of great poetry to labor camp or the gallows?

The words are in jest, but the intensity of the indignation is enormous.

I believe that, unconsciously, he divided all humanity not according to whether they were "good" or "evil," but according to whether they were talented or untalented. And not just in art, but in general.

Dividing people in this way was especially characteristic of him when he was young. I can remember it from my childhood.

A carpenter from the Olonetsky province named Mikhaila arrived to install a new fence and porch steps, and no matter how often people told him that Mikhaila was a scoundrel and a thief—he'd stolen a saw from one person, a pail from someone else—Kornei Ivanovich only waved away the complaints.

"Just listen to the way he speaks! Every word's a delight, every story, a *bylina*!"* (Having spent his boyhood and adolescence in Odessa, Kornei Ivanovich hated the local southern dialect; everything from word choice to syntax and pronunciation seemed to him not only incorrect, but intolerably vulgar: "Daeymon" for "demon" or "Odeyessa"—he'd draw out the vowels, imitating a young woman from Odessa.

"You go and 'we'll come on along later [*podoidyem*]' or even 'follow on after [*nadoidyem*],'" he'd say, teasing his friends from Odessa who came to visit us in Kuokkala. It's still a puzzle to me how he managed in three or four years to remove from his speech—once and for all—any trace of his Odessa childhood and youth and to develop his rich, strong, irreproachable Moscow-Petersburg Russian. He spoke beautiful Ukrainian, the language of his mother Ekaterina Osipovna, and could recite almost all Shevchenko's poetry by heart; and he knew the fine points of both literary and colloquial Russian. Knew them and loved them.)

"Mikhaila here told me yesterday how they build their huts up north. Just imagine what they call the main beam in the hut—'the mother beam.' 'The mother' (he smiled with delight). And the window casings, rafters,

---

*Traditional folk epic in song form, plural *byliny*. (Translator)

and carved fretwork? Why, every word of his is fretwork. You tell me to fire him. For me he's a festive occasion. With his hatchet, his saw, his language—he's a virtuoso."

Mikhaila was an artist; he wore the halo of immunity.

Kornei Ivanovich was so accustomed to dividing people into the inspired and talented and the mechanical, mediocre, and untalented, that he would apply the terms to circumstances and occurrences seemingly not at all related to talent.

Speaking of the weather: "It's brilliant here right now." Rain at an inconvenient time poured with a hopeless lack of talent. On a bright sunny day he might say: "The weather today is God-inspired."

To a friend: "How untalented of you not to be with us last Sunday."

Of himself: "What an unfortunate mediocrity I am, I missed the train today..."

He was extraordinarily sensitive to talent and the lack of it in pedagogy, in both education and child-rearing. He demanded from a teacher both enthusiasm for his subject and the ability to encourage and fascinate his students. He despised teachers who couldn't even interest children in Pushkin, who burdened them instead of delighting them. He despised teachers and parents who resorted to drill. He even claimed the existence of a rule that the less inspired the adult, the greater his passion for training: "Sonya, don't wiggle your legs so!" "Vitya, how can you sit that way?" "Sit up straight!" "Now what did I say? Wash your hands!"

Children themselves love to be commanded (that's why commands are part of a game), but commanded inventively, amusingly, not seargent-major style.

Not for one minute did he doubt the ineptitude, the out-and-out criminality of adults who beat children. The perversion of Tyutchev or Baratynsky, in his exaggerated style, merited "hanging" or a "term at hard labor ..." What then the man who raised his hand against a child?

"...with more reverence for children, and less arrogance," he wrote in a 1911 article, "you will open for yourself treasures of wisdom, beauty and spiritual grace beyond your wildest imaginings."[4]

"Treasures of wisdom, beauty and spiritual grace"—he's speaking about children here, not Pushkin or Baratynsky.

"...a child's games and fun are the most sacred things of all."[5]

He pulled Kolya and me out of the Kuokkala gymnasium suddenly and decisively. Our studies were going all right, not well, not badly, but I made an unexpected discovery—Alexei Nikolaevich, our director, a ruddy man with a toothy smile who was always very nice to parents, beat children on the sly.

On my way home from school one day, I remembered that I'd left my hood hanging on a coathook and went back to get it. There in the cloakroom I saw Alexei Nikolaevich, screened by the clothes rack, holding Kostya Rassadin's head between his knees and whipping him with a belt. He was beating him evenly, blow after blow, methodically, almost indifferently. Most terrifying of all, he was holding Kostya's mouth shut with his hand.

I closed the door as quietly as I could and set off at a run. I returned home without my hood. I was so terrified that I began to stutter as I described what I'd seen—and stuttered for several days afterwards. I talked and talked about it, I couldn't be calmed, yet I couldn't explain just what it was that had so upset me. After all, I'd seen boys fight, or mothers on the beach slap their offspring, or fathers cuff the backs of their heads; I had even seen the coachman Kollyari lash our friend Pavka's bare legs with the reins, making him jump and howl with pain.

But all that had been done out of anger, irritation, strong feeling. This was the first time I'd ever seen one person beat another methodically, calmly, virtually whistling as he did so—especially an adult a child.

I was almost ill with shock.

One person listening to me would say, "What cruelty!"

Another: "The boy deserved it; he was a second-year student and a hooligan."

A third: "Beating children in gymnasium is against the law."

"What mediocrity!" said Kornei Ivanovich with disgust. "Good-for-nothing!"

As I learned later, he wrote a letter to the director and a complaint to the Ministry of Education. He explained that a director who beat children had to be evil-tempered and untalented, and an untalented, mediocre director could hardly be capable of choosing talented colleagues. Quite the opposite: untalented people always dislike and persecute talented people.

Withdrawing us from the gymnasium, Kornei Ivanovich began, along with Vera Mikhailovna, to teach us himself—Russian history as well as English. Not us, really, but Kolya, who had just turned eleven. I was free to hang about, however, and Boba stuck around, too—he didn't like not being allowed to do things.

Vera Mikhailovna taught Kolya by the textbook, closely following the gymnasium curriculum; Kornei Ivanovich taught "sort of," "in general," "freely."

He told stories about events and people. As I now understand, he chose occasions, episodes, events, important historical figures (primarily of the nineteenth century), which were the most dramatic and gave us the richest food for our imaginations and emotions, those which one could reenact, play out. Pages from Karamzin, Klyuchevsky, retold or read aloud; monologues from the historical dramas and tragedies of Pushkin or Alexei Tolstoy; reproductions of historical paintings; excerpts from Herzen's *My Past and Thoughts*—descriptions of the heroes of the Decembrist revolt, Tsar Nicholas, Benckendorff, Dubbelt and Arakcheev, sometimes in Herzen's emotional style, sometimes sarcastically.

Naturally, poetry played a part in these lessons. In his recitations, no matter what the aim, poetry remained poetry; the poems sounded the same in his study as they did on the sea, but the goal was different. Here he chose them to illustrate some event or other: discussing Prince Vladimir, he'd recite Alexei Tolstoy's "Ilya Muromets;" Peter the Great's decision to build a city on the Finnish swamp called for Maikov's "Who is He?;" when discussion turned to the war with Sweden, he'd thunder "Poltava," but not before he'd explained all the names to us:

> There's Sheremétev, noble earl,
> And Bruce, and Baur, and Repnin,
> And he, low-born but fortune's pearl,
> Half chancellor, half sovereign.[6]

The conversation turns to the lycée—he reads next the poem, "October 19," but not before we know what became of each lycée student, those mentioned as well as those not mentioned, the colleagues of Pushkin: Matyushkin (the future admiral), Gorchakov (future diplomat), Delvig (poet), Pushchin and Küchelbecker (participants in the Decembrist uprising)—not before we know who is the subject of each line.

As we listen, we delightedly guess that these lines describe Matyushkin:

> . . . From the threshold of the lycée
> You to a ship quick with a laugh did spring,
> And from that time, the sea's your constant roadway,
> O favorite son of wave and wind![7]

We learn about Pushkin's exile in Mikhailovskoe and Pushchin's visit with him there—and only then:

> My oldest friend, companion peerless!
> I too blessed fate when far up north
> In my retreat remote and cheerless,
> Adrift in dismal snow, so fearless
> Your little sleigh bell tinkled forth.[8]

The Decembrist uprising, Pushchin's exile in Siberia, Pushkin's chance meeting with Küchelbecker on the road as Küchelbecker was being taken off to the fortress-prison:

> Like friend embracing friend in silence
> Before his banishment so cruel. . .[9]

and Pushchin's words in 1837 when the news of Pushkin's death reached him in Siberia: he, Pushchin, would gladly have shielded the poet with his own breast if he had been in Petersburg. . . I repeat, Kornei Ivanovich recited poetry during our lessons to illustrate the events on Senate Square or the opening of the Lycée, but most often poetry served as the final sentence on an event or a person—the sentence of history pronounced by the lips of a poet. The conclusion of the musical phrase served to conclude the historical drama: Pushkin on the Decembrists in Siberia, Lermontov on the death of Pushkin, Nekrasov on the death of Shevchenko.

> Do not give way to excessive lamenting:
> This was foreseen by us, almost desirable.
> Thus meets his death by the Lord's sacred blessing
> On Russian soil a man most remarkable. . . [10]

The same tragic theme, fundamental to his understanding of art, appeared everywhere in his narratives: the unremitting attack on genius and talent by the powerful, massed forces of mediocrity.

This was always a painful issue for him.

The desecration of talent. The persecution of talent. The ongoing struggle of defenseless talent against well-armed talentlessness.

One day he read us Leskov's tale *Lefty,* a terrible but amusing story about some English craftsmen who create a marvel, a clockwork flea. Russian artisans shoe this wonder of wonders—imagine making shoes for almost invisible feet!—and then some brutal soldiers kill the master of masters, the ingenious *Lefty.*

(Not long ago, in 1970, I had the chance to see a letter from Kornei Ivanovich to the artist Nikolai Vasilyevich Kuzmin thanking him for a copy of a new edition of Leskov's tale which Kuzmin had illustrated.

Kornei Ivanovich admired the illustrations enormously.

As I read Chukovsky's letter to Kuzmin, written so many years after and so many miles away from Kuokkala, I see clearly in my mind's eye the bookshelves at Kuokkala, flooded with cold winter sunshine, the whiter than white field of snow sparkling outside the window, and the lean, young, dark-haired Kornei Ivanovich sitting in the middle of the sofa, all sharp knees and long, thin, restless fingers.

He is reading us *Lefty.*

Kolya is sitting crosslegged at one end of the sofa, listening quietly; I lie at the other end, head on the round arm, flinching with each kick aimed at Lefty. Our teacher sits at the table. She listens attentively; of course she'd prefer us to be sitting up straight on chairs in proper scholarly fashion, not lounging on the sofa; but by now she understands that things aren't done in the "correct" way at this house, and she doesn't grumble.

I see the sofa, the window sparkling with rosy-blue winter radiance, and the nervous hands and knees of the reader. He is reading to us about the destruction of a man of genius and all the untalented lackeys who destroyed him.)

Why, almost a century later in 1970, do I remember so clearly the reading on that long ago winter's day in Kuokkala?

I have read Kornei Ivanovich's letter to Nikolai Vassilyevich Kuzmin: Kornei Ivanovich writes that with his illustrations the artist has revealed the main theme of the story, "how people of greatness are trampled down."

Kornei Ivanovich's history lessons at Kuokkala were suffused with this same familiar, painful theme.

The murder of Lermontov. He was murdered by untalented mediocrities in league together, as was Pushkin, as was Lefty.

"Think of it, that cretin Nicholas could have calmly sent Pushkin off to Siberia in 1825! To that place where he sent the most talented people in Russia! And we would have been deprived of 'Poltava' and *Eugene Onegin*! He and all his Kleinmichels and Benckendorffs—they simply didn't have the capacity for appreciating art! They killed Pushkin in 1837—one can't begin to imagine what else he might have written, what else he might have bequeathed to us!"

I was born in 1907. I couldn't possibly have remembered the revolution of 1905. But somehow it always seemed to me, seems to me now, that I remember it; that's undoubtedly because all the adults who surrounded us when we were children talked about it as if they'd been witnesses or participants.

Kornei Ivanovich visited the *Potemkin* when the mutinous ship was moored in Odessa; later, in Petersburg, he became the editor of *Signal*, a satirical magazine ridiculing the tsarist regime, its ministers, and its most "august" personage. ("Nicholas the Second was the least talented of all the Russian tsars," he said.) He talked to us about Lieutenant Schmidt, Sevastopol, and Presnya, but most often of all—about the ninth of January in Petersburg.* He drew us a map of the city streets, bridges, boulevards; the workers with banners and portraits of the tsar walk along these bridges and boulevards to the Winter Palace, but soldiers and cossacks lie in wait for them, hidden in courtyards and sidestreets. The people are going to tell their little father, the tsar, how evil people "trample on them," they who live in basements, in poverty and servitude, working twelve hours a day for

---

*Russia's humiliating defeat in the Russo-Japanese war (1904–5) set off the uprisings known as the revolution of 1905. These included Bloody Sunday in St. Petersburg on 9 January 1905, the mutiny of the cruiser Potemkin in Odessa in June, the mutiny of Lieutenant Schmidt in Sevastopol in November, and street fighting in the Krasnaya Presnya region of Moscow in December. (Translator)

54

pennies; but they are met by cossacks, whips, bullets, and now upon the white snow (I look out at the untouched white blanket beyond the window) lie pools of blood and unmoving corpses, arms and legs flung wide.

In other lessons during that memorable winter, Kornei Ivanovich told us about the duel in which Pushkin was killed (horses, sleighs, snow, the pistol in D'Anthes's hand), concluding his story by reading Lermontov. After all the rhythmic twists and turns, mournful, angry, threatening, he triumphantly and solemnly ended:

> In vain to calumny you'll turn for your salvation:
> 'Twill help no more, and all the flood
> Of your black blood shall ne'er bring expiation
> For the poet's righteous, holy blood![11]

This was the first blood I saw in my imagination, the sacred red blood of the poet on the white snow.

Maybe because our teacher unconsciously conveyed to us his secret belief that a poet's murderer is also a murderer of the people; or maybe because both evil events—the murder of Pushkin and the shooting of the demonstrators—took place in January in the snow on similar sounding dates, one on the ninth, the other on the twenty-ninth, they became permanently and indissolubly linked in my memory. The blood of the poet and the blood of the people marching to the palace on January ninth. The thought of both these January days, decades apart, with no apparent connection to each other, direct or indirect, can still make my heart contract with the same sharp, sudden pain I first felt back then in my childhood.

(Maybe it's because he told us about both events in the same voice? I don't know. But D'Anthes's shot and the shots of January ninth to this day ring out for me with one and the same sound.)

CHAPTER

IX

"My children were fortunate: from their earliest years, art was in the air they breathed," said Kornei Ivanovich to one of his numerous Peredelkino visitors, who had brought to him her poetry-writing daughter.

Truly, we were fortunate. Our good fortune was due to the fact that Kornei Ivanovich couldn't spend a single day without literature, without the society of artistic and literary friends; and when we were small, we were underfoot willy-nilly when his friends were around.

We were hardly ever taken to Petersburg or Vyborg, except to visit the dentist or buy a coat. I was ten or eleven before I visited a real theater, in Petrograd* after we'd left Kuokkala (and after the revolution!). Kornei Ivanovich did take us to the Alexander III Museum twice while we lived at the dacha, to show us the work of Rokotov, Borovikovsky, Bryullov, Serov, and Repin. He also took us to the Hermitage, but the columns, the parquet floors, and the view of the Neva and the Peter Paul Fortress crowded Titian and Rubens into the background for me. All I remembered from my first trip to the Hermitage were the Egyptian scarabs. There were albums of reproductions at home which I looked through on winter evenings but never opened during the summer.

But it was probably not objets d'art, which were altogether few in our house, but literally the air we breathed which Kornei Ivanovich meant when he said we were fortunate.

We lived diagonally across from Penates, and ran back and forth with notes from Kornei Ivanovich to Ilya Efimovich almost every day. Sometimes we were in Repin's studio to hear his remarks to his students or the judgments of artists and writers on Repin's canvases. Whether at Penates, at

---

*The city of St. Petersburg was renamed Petrograd in 1914, and Leningrad in 1924. (Translator)

home, or on the beach, we were surrounded by the joys, sorrows, and delights of literary people.

Kornei Chukovsky wrote about his relations with members of the art world—the close, long-term, enduring ones as well as the brief and superficial ones—in his book *Contemporaries* and in other writings. His memoirs are a portrait gallery, some full-length renderings, others sketches done in a few swift strokes. Repin, Mayakovsky, Gorky, Tynyanov, Anna Akhmatova, Bunin, Kuprin, Tatiana Shepkina-Kupernik, N.F. Annensky, Korolenko, Innokenty Annensky, T. Bogdanovich, Tarle, Koni, Leonid Andreev, Kvitko, Zhitkov, Marshak.

A good half of these are the people he spent time with in Kuokkala.

He felt at home among the literati, relaxed and natural, although not on an equal footing because, as I have already said, he considered himself devoid of that crucial attribute he so revered in others—artistic genius, talent. (All his life he only admitted to one personal quality: industriousness.)

"What kind of writer am I?"—yet he could not and would not for one minute live without literary work or outside literary and artistic circles. And he was delighted that we, his children, from our earliest years breathed this same cherished air.

The fact that we did not consider our father and our surroundings special or exceptional was certainly due to the way he raised us.

If it sometimes occurred to us that our father and his friends differed from the dachniks who spent their summers in Kuokkala, the difference lay in the idleness of the dachniks and the intense busyness of Kornei Ivanovich, his friends and acquaintances.

The air of art was more than anything the air of hard work. Kornei Ivanovich and his friends occasionally relaxed, but they were never idle.

Relaxation and idleness do not resemble each other at all. Improvised lectures in a gazebo at Repin's, the reciting of poetry, conversation, debate, skittles and other games, mostly literary ones, were all included in the air around us, but not a grain of intellectual idleness. In the studio, in the study, on the beach (I suspect even in dreams) Kornei Ivanovich and his circle continued the work of spirit and mind so vital to their existence. The recreational pursuits of the people around us in no way resembled the diversions of the dachniks, especially the ladies, who could spend whole days on the beach turning themselves from one side to the other with complete seriousness, dip into the sea three steps from the water's edge, shrieking loudly (for what fun is a dip without a shriek!), then in the evenings parade back and forth on the station platform in expectation of unexpected meetings.

The relations between the residents of Penates and our house were close and strong. Guests from Penates, from the park with the intricate gazebos, flowerbeds, and little bridges, from the roomy, sprawling house with its glass roof, porches, and sets of stairs, from the dining room with its famous round table (a great circle crowned with a smaller one which revolved and was covered with vegetarian dishes)—guests from Penates, crossing the Big Road and strolling along the seashore, would walk onto the totally unremarkable Chukovsky shorefront, where the only thing one could call intricate were the uncut roots which snaked along the ground; and they'd sit down to tea at a most ordinary square-cornered table with the most ordinary things to eat. Or the opposite would occur: Kornei Ivanovich would take a writer, poet, or critic who'd come to visit him over to Penates, to meet Repin. And Kolya and I would tag along after them.

Kornei Ivanovich was treated like a member of the household at Penates. Repin became very attached to him during the year they were neighbors. Not a single Repin "Wednesday," not a single entertainment organized "for the folk" at Penates or at the "Prometheus" theater took place without Kornei Ivanovich's participation, and if Kornei Ivanovich was late, Repin would impatiently send one of his grandchildren or his students to tell him: "Hurry up!" Ilya Efimovich loved to have Kornei Ivanovich read to him when he was working or relaxing—Pushkin's, Nekrasov's or Shevchenko's poetry, the prose of Gogol or Lermontov, or sometimes something new, resoundingly modern; he loved to have Kornei Ivanovich recite for his guests at the dining room table or out in the open; he showed him new versions of his pictures; he entrusted him with the editing of his memoirs . . . Chukovsky, quite naturally, became one of Repin's links with the younger literary generation.

The furnishings in each house were different, and tastes and opinions differed (due to the disparity in age, if for no other reason). But though the way of life differed from house to house, the topics of conversation, dictated by the events of the day, were the same. They talked about the religious teachings of Tolstoy and his excommunication from the Church, about his departure from Yasnaya* and about his death . . . (A photograph of Repin and Natalia Borisovna with Chukovsky and my mother in Repin's studio has been preserved and hangs before my eyes at this very moment in Peredelkino—on the wall in the background is a portrait of Tolstoy having breakfast with Sophia Andreevna as well as an unfinished portrait of Kornei Chukovsky; Ilya Efimovich is holding the newspaper in which for the first time Tolstoy's face appears framed in black.)

. . . Strange that I, a three-and-a-half-year-old girl, should clearly remember that day, or perhaps not that one but the day before: the moment when Kornei Ivanovich, upon learning that Tolstoy had died, laid his head in his big hands on the table and wept.

The photograph, it seems to me, was taken the following day.

---

*Yasnaya Polyana, the ancestral estate which Tolstoy always considered his home. (Translator)

Looking at it now, I can see the puzzled grief on each face—a lack of preparedness for the new, just-begun age, the sort of expression which must have been on Gogol's face when in his letter to Pletnev he exclaimed: "Russia without Pushkin!"—"How strange! God, how strange. Russia without Pushkin."

The words seem to say—can this be Russia?

The death of Pushkin burst upon people unexpectedly; the death of Tolstoy had been anticipated from day to day; yet all the same people were unprepared.

"Russia without Tolstoy! How strange! God, how strange!"

Can this be Russia?

Kornei Ivanovich went to the funeral.

...In both houses there was talk of Socialist Revolutionary bombings, the shooting of the strikers on the River Lena, and other events of a political and social nature; sometimes they'd collect money, sometimes provide secret refuge for political runaways who'd crossed the Finnish border; after August 1914 they spoke about the war, the war, the war, about fighting at the Carpathian Mountains and the Mazurian Lakes, about what the consequences of the war might be; but in both places there was no end to the discussion of books, pictures, actors, stage productions, magazines. Chaliapin. Korolenko. Vrubel. Komissarzhevskaya. Serov. Blok. Sologub. Futurists. Acmeists. Mayakovsky. Akhmatova. Bryusov. Puni. Kulbin. The Art Theater. Evreinov. Meyerhold. Boris Grigoriev. Dobuzhinsky. Bakst. *Russian Wealth. The World of Art. Russian Thought. The Scales. Apollon.*

Did we listen to these conversations? No. (To tell the truth, because we were young and intellectually lazy, we were sometimes even bored by them. Sometimes we even envied the hated dachniks: they had nameday and birthday parties, guests came to visit them at any and all times, their homes were not bewitched, as ours was, by the two words: "Papa's working.")

No, in those days, we certainly did not always think of ourselves as "fortunate."

However, whether we wished to or no, we breathed the air which filled our house. And thanks to Kornei Ivanovich's mocking nature, his good taste and his desire to avoid mawkishness and baby talk, our environment did not turn us into conceited child prodigies.

Kornei Ivanovich couldn't bear child prodigies, and most particularly, parents who showed off their children's talents. A little girl with ribbons around her curls set by mama and papa on a chair in the center of the room reciting for the entertainment of guests:

> Cornflowers on the verges
> Are very sweet to see[1]

60

or singing, to general laughter, a bawdy couplet whose meaning everyone but her understands—these Deribasovsky Street* ways were definitely alien to our house. (I only learned of their existence much later.) No one ever said to anyone in our presence that Lidochka had composed a very promising little verse at the age of three:

> A frying pan is handy,
> If you want to cook up brandy,

or that Kolichka, dissatisfied with the way the children in Chekhov's story "The Boys" had given up their daring plans to run away, had, to show them up, begun to write "My Remembrances of California."

Kornei Ivanovich loved children's amusements, but would not tolerate adults amusing themselves at the expense of children.

Vulgarity was nonexistent in the air we breathed.

Nor was it polluted by rank-consciousness and arrogance, any more than by idleness.

The official Table of Ranks had no meaning in our house. We had absolutely no idea, for instance, that Repin held the rank of Privy Councillor or that Koni, too, had some sort of title and had been awarded decorations. Petersburg artistic circles, which also influenced Kuokkala, had their own scale of values. What Privy or State Councillor title or order of Anne at neck or lapel could eclipse the glow of the names Komissarzhevskaya, Serov, Repin, Korolenko, Gorky? Anna Akhmatova? Blok?

These people were wonderfully able to admire each other. "I am ready to kiss the hands of the artist"—such a level of admiration was not unusual among them. Historians of Russian culture have long since explored in detail all the feuds and disagreements between the schools, between representatives of different artistic trends at the beginning of the century. Disagreements on principle as well as personal quarrels. That's good: without such research history would be vague, confused, just plain false. But I wish to recall here one of the worthy traits characteristic of the best people of the epoch: their ability to admire that miracle of existence which is called artistic genius.

Take, for example, Repin's telegram to Chaliapin sent in response to the news that Chaliapin was planning to come to Penates (1914): "Paschally exultant; house, studio, canvases, paints, artist ready, Monday, Tuesday, Wednesday. Is this a dream? Repin."[2]

Is this a dream? With such a question one might end a letter to one's beloved. Was it really possible to see Chaliapin again, to welcome him at his

---

*A main street in Odessa. (Translator)

own house, to work on his portrait! What happiness! The joyful ringing of harness bells is almost audible in this telegram.

Or this: Blok and Stanislavsky have a meeting for which they have high hopes. The meeting is totally unsuccessful.

Blok had suggested that Stanislavsky put on his just-completed play, *The Rose and the Cross*, at the Art Theater. The author pinned all his hopes on Stanislavsky. Here is the entry from his diary:

> April 20, 1913.
> ...If he wants to, he can both put on the play and himself act the role of Bertran. If *his genius touches the play*, I will not worry about anything else. Stanislavsky's mistakes are as enormous as his successes. *If he himself isn't interested*—then I'm in the "dumps" again, no one else can help.[3]

The attempt was a failure.

After numerous conversations, Blok was discouraged and felt that Stanislavsky did not understand the play. He expected adverse reaction. But here's the entry:

> April 29
> ...a sensitive person came to see me, a person in whom I believe, who has done great things (Chekhov at the Art Theater) and *he understood nothing, "grasped" nothing, felt nothing.* That means I'll be writing "under a bushel" again.[4]

Bitter lines, but Blok did not lose his respect or love for Stanislavsky.

Even after sharp, sometimes violent quarrels on the debate platform or on the page of a magazine, it was still possible to admire intensely the achievement, talent, greatness of another person. People of widely differing opinions sensed their membership in a mutual brotherhood of culture and continued to love each other.

The fruit of this unity in diversity was *Chukokkala*.

Strolling with his guests along the damp sand at the sea's edge, sitting with them on his veranda or in Repin's studio, Kornei Ivanovich undertook to preserve the voices and footprints. He started an album of drawings and autographs.

Repin gave the project a name, combining the first part of the owner's family name "Chuk" with the ending of the name of the hamlet "okkala."

I was lucky: I remember *Chukokkala* not only in its magnificent, voluminous old age, but also in the days when it was young and slim.

A modest rectangular notebook with a cover done by the artist A. Arnshtam. Chukovsky, cap on his head, thin knees to his chin, sits on the shore of the bay with the cherished notebook in his hands. A line of long-haired artists stretches toward him on the shore, while boats come sailing across the water: clearly, writers and poets roost there.

At the top of the cover, the inscription: "To Kornei Chukovsky. Shevchenko's own successor and co-thinker, the cream of art now may you skim and drink here. B. Sadovskoy."

Many were the times I watched Kornei Ivanovich show off his treasures. His long fingers would open the notebook and lightly, lightly flip through the pages. The public exhibitions of *Chukokkala* were veritable one-man theatricals. Grandly, keeping his distance, not allowing the album out of his hands, turning first to one side then the other in front of the guests seated dress-circle-like on the sofa, Kornei Ivanovich would show off a new Repin drawing, calling out, as if in advertisement, when and why the drawing had been made, its brilliant artistic merits, its highpoints.

"If fat began to trickle off the page onto the tablecloth right now, it would mean that stupidity itself had begun to drip. Each eyebrow here is a dope, and the chin—look at it—what an idiot! And the fat flesh, the cheeks, neck and ears, that is not fatness of flesh, but fatness of soul! The artist has presented us with a fattened human soul!"

Having given his guests a chance to savor the skill of the artist and the fatty stupidity of his chance model, Kornei Ivanovich would move to some new achievement in gymnastic versifying: here the names "Maria Chukovskaya" and "Kornei Chukovsky" were crossed in the middle of a madrigal written by Gumilyov; and here were four impromptus, the second of which makes fun of the first, the third and fourth—of both previous ones.

...Now *Chukokkala* is a memorial to an age that has passed, a memorial in which time stands still and every line and every comma has become set, has become history, as hard as bronze or marble, as befits a memorial; once upon a time it was something alive, fleeting, elusive, delicate, constantly changing its outlines, like tobacco smoke, maybe, or the tinkling of a spoon in a teacup. *Chukokkala* was, if you like, a solid and condensed version of that "air of art" which, in the words of Kornei Ivanovich, we were fortunate enough to breathe as children.

This air has been preserved to the present day on the open pages of an album, not closed up in a jar. It has not flown off. It has not blown away.

Chukokkala celebrated "the sharp-edged humor of the literary joke."[5] But the humor and wit, qualities of any artistic society in any age, did not drown out a different sound, the sound of an approaching storm, soon to break. The more the killingly funny tricks, brain-teasing, rhyming conundrums, joking squabbles, and competitions in witty slander and caricature in *Chukokkala*, the more clearly sound from its pages the tragic and serious voices of Leonid Andreev, Gorky, Repin, Akhmatova, Blok.

There are as many amusing impromptus as anyone could ask:

Before me right now fin
And lettuce.
But at this min
I'm surplus.

And then—making fun of that impromptu and its author:

Before me right now lettuce
And fin
No, I'm not surplus
At this min.

And then—this mournful observation:

At the Chukokuokkalsky's own den,
O, fairmindedness, you're gone again.

And then—this impassioned reproach to the director Evreinov for his mocking reshaping of the first impromptu. The reproach is a play on words: Evrei-nov and Evrei-old.

Evrei! the old law: don't steal,*
To Evréinóv is sure unknown.—
O, theatrical caprice full-blown,
You've turned honor on its heel.

All this was a month before the beginning of the war. Leafing ahead a few pages:

8 August 1914.
Now in one great theater there plays but one great tragedy—the war...
                    Leonid Andreev

Then in a different time, a completely different, new time after the war, during the revolution, in Petrograd, not Kuokkala, I notice the firm hand-writing of Blok on the pages of the *Chukokkala* notebook and, uncomprehending, read a few lines he penned, following a four-line stanza I knew by heart:

---

*The phrase "old law" can also mean Old Testament and extends the pun on the name Evreinov because "Evrei" in Russian means Jew. (Translator)

64

In hottest of summers, in winter's cruel raging,
On days of your weddings, successes, last rites—
To scare off my mood, so deathly despairing
I wait for a sound, yet unheard, very light...

Such is the "artist"—and it's still true, there's nothing to do, art
and life cannot be reconciled.

13 March 1919

At a meeting.

Alexander Blok.[6]

It cannot—or—can it?

This entry, however, takes my story too far ahead; it was written when
the Kuokkala seashore was already behind us, and *Chukokkala* had begun
to suffer many ordeals and adventures. Kornei Ivanovich wrote about them
himself; I will mention only one of the last: in the fall of 1941, long after
Penates and the dacha at Kuokkala, Kornei Ivanovich hastily buried *Chukokkala* in his yard at Peredelkino when he was rushing back and forth between Moscow and Peredelkino in preparation for evacuation to Tashkent.
This effort to save the album didn't turn out very well: the neighbor's yardman, hoping for diamonds or gold, dug up the buried treasure and, much
disappointed, used a number of pages for cigarette wrappers.

The rest survived thanks to the chance return of their owner.

And now (also totally by chance!) I am probably the only one left on earth
who remembers another (by no means the only) lost *Chukokkala* page: an
entry and drawing done by Repin at the end of February 1917:*

"Today the soldier looked as if he had been taken up to heaven alive." And
accompanying these words: shoulders, bayonet, and a happy, almost childlike peasant's face turned up to the sky.

...The close ties between our house and Penates, which lasted for so
many years, were varied in nature, both artistic and everyday. We went to
Repin's to get water from the artesian well. Kolya and I were sometimes
taken to the studio, and Kolya occasionally even to the "Wednesdays." (The
other well from which we, not knowing it ourselves, drew fresh water.) Repin painted portraits of Kornei Ivanovich and Maria Borisovna. He even
started one of me, but didn't finish it. No matter what happened, good or
bad, we'd go to Repin's. His studio was a spiritual center. Tolstoy died: everyone gathered at Repin's. Mayakovsky appeared: he absolutely must be introduced to Repin. Misfortune strikes—Repin. One memory: Kolya,

---

*The time of the revolution of February 1917 during which Tsar Nicholas II abdi-
cated and the autocracy was replaced by a democratic Provisional Government.
(Translator)

covered with blood, stands in our small kitchen near the water barrel, and Papa pours pitcher after pitcher, pitcher after pitcher of cold water over his head. The water is all bloody. "Run to Repin's," he cries, catching sight of me. "They've torn Kolya's ear with a stone, ask for the horse—to go to the hospital." I rush off, and at the gate his shouted command overtakes me: "If Ilya Efimovich is working, don't bother him, find Vera Ilyinichna." I race on as fast as I can, praying God Ilya Efimovich is not working because we're afraid of Vera Ilyinichna. What luck! I meet Ilya Efimovich right at the gates of Penates about to set off on a walk. He immediately turns around and hurries to the yardman's lodge, and I, back home. The carriage, going at top speed, passes me on the Big Road, and by the time I get to our gate, Kolya is already seated in the carriage, a towel round his head, Mama and Papa on either side of him.

That evening Ilya Efimovich himself came by to let us know that the patient was all right and his injured ear had been sewed up successfully.

Repin's appearance was always preceded by a few minutes by the appearance of Mik, his old, one-eyed, curly-haired poodle, which, it seems to me, they never had trimmed; he was completely round.

Mik's sniffing around the gate. That means Repin's about to appear.

And there he is, in his gray suit, rather dry, gray-haired, not very tall. He asks after Kolya, then sits down for fifteen minutes and during those fifteen minutes draws our visiting neighbor with quick, little strokes on a small gray pad he takes from his pocket.

I watch from behind his back. He doesn't lift his eyes from his subject.

His hand moves quickly, obedient to his glance.

Repin hardly ever glances at his paper or pencil, only over there at her face.

It's as if an invisible wire stretches between her face and his hand.

CHAPTER

X

More than half a century has passed since the time I have been describing. What a lot has been written since then about the first decades of this century! And, in particular, about Repin and Penates! Two thick volumes of *Artistic Heritage* are devoted entirely to Repin; many pages to the "Wednesdays;" whole volumes to Chaliapin, Gorky, and Mayakovsky. Biographical "works and days" and books of annotated correspondence were compiled long ago. It would have been worth my while to page through these books in order to arm myself with basic information about the beliefs, habits, disagreements, friendships, and quarrels of all the writers, artists, and performers who stepped off the dacha train at the Kuokkala Station of the Finland Railway, mostly on Wednesdays and Sundays, from 1906, when Kornei Ivanovich first settled there, until the fall of 1917, when he left for Petrograd.

But I am writing reminiscences, not biography and certainly not history. I can remember bits and pieces from 1910 on, that is, from the time I was three. What can a child between the ages of three and ten remember? Not a great deal; not in order; not clearly; however, though few and vague, these memories have value insofar as they are true, independent, and one's own.

That being the case, meager as they are, they may be of some use to others.

Awakened, my memory seems remarkably childish. Of all those distinguished people who visited our house on Sundays, and occasionally other days, it has retained not the main characteristics, only secondary ones, not the important details, only incidental ones; not the things about an illustrious person which make him interesting to an adult, but those which make any passerby interesting to a child. If a person walks by with a dog on a chain, any child is interested first in the dog, and only later in the human being. The horse whose silky coat you pat as a child and whom you feed sugar from the palm of your hand is unforgettable. And as for the first squirrel!

Mayakovsky was probably the only exception. He's the only one I remember in his major capacity—as a poet—not in some lesser way. Maybe that was because Kornei Ivanovich specifically prepared us to be able to appreciate poetry. Maybe it was because Mayakovsky had practically no secondary or side characteristics.

I remember that he always came to our house from the direction of the sea and that he would stride along the shore, composing verses out loud, on the row of stones where Kolya usually jumped.

In 1915 Mayakovsky drew a picture of me—I was eight then; he probably sensed how eagerly I listened to him.

Yes, I loved his defiantly scornful, always thunderous recitations—whether he was reciting for a large group or for Kornei Ivanovich alone (Kolya and I didn't count).

What did he seem like to me then, how did I see him and what do I remember?

In order to recall as clearly as possible my own vision of him at the time, I must turn to lines written by someone else with no reference to Mayakovsky whatsoever. The lines were written by Blok, and I read them much later. They didn't, couldn't have the slightest relation to Mayakovsky—they're from Blok's love poems!—but as soon as I read or recall them, I see Mayakovsky as he was then in Kuokkala, on the green Kuokkala sofa or on the rocks by the sea, dropping his eyes solemnly just before beginning to recite.

Here are the lines from Blok:

(That's the way lions look at people
Morosely staring through their fence.)[1]

When Mayakovsky recited, the look in his serious eyes was always morose, if not threatening. And always from behind an invisible fence. All around him were people; he belonged to some different species.

You know, I pity the poor Peruvian.
Stupid to give him the galleys.
Judges just bother the bird, and the dance,
And me, and you, and Peru.[2]

I envied him so haughtily judging judges and felt uncomfortable for myself, as if I were among those he was judging.

And then there were my favorite lines:

And faded then in a moment the peacock's
Thoroughly splendid tail![3]

68

The words "faded then in a moment" he pronounced momentarily, but "thoroughly splendid," slowly and importantly, as if unfurling the whole, fanlike, splendid peacock's tail.

But I was eight years old, and I must admit it wasn't only Mayakovsky's poems that interested me. Every bit as much as I loved listening to poetry, I loved to watch the way he played croquet. I tagged after him every time he set out for the croquet green at our close friends' and nearest neighbors, the Bogdanoviches—Tatiana Alexandrovna, my godmother, and her children, Shura, Sonya, Volodya, and Tanya. The lionlikeness, the moroseness, the fence disappear; he's just a young man playing croquet with some teenage girls, but even here he's passionate and absolutely invincible. Everyone else holds the mallet with two hands and bends over, but he, though taller than anyone else, doesn't bow toward the ball at all and holds his mallet in one hand. He holds it like a walking stick, hits the ball surely, is always the first to become poison, and when he's poison—what fun it is to watch: how the balls fly, how they crack! His power over the mallet and balls seemed magical to me. Naturally, I wasn't included in the game; I was happy if I got the chance to give Mayakovsky back a ball which had flown beyond the edge of the croquet lawn. My level of understanding was so primitive that when Tatiana Alexandrovna said to Sonya one day: "It would be better if you didn't play with Vladimir Vladimirovich today, Sonyusha, your stroke's off," I took her literally: "Her stroke's off—Sonya's weak today, she's not capable of hitting the ball."

Repin. The studio. I remember the canvases on their easels, many Pushkins, a Chaliapin, I remember some kind of dark, sunburned people boldly rowing a wide boat across the waves. I remember Repin at Kornei Ivanovich's desk drawing someone in *Chukokkala* with a cigarette butt, which he dipped into the inkwell. But I was seven, and more than about portraits, pictures, brushes, canvases, and such strange implements as a cigarette butt, I wondered if it was really true what they said about Repin's Mik going after a live chicken in our neighbor's yard not long ago, and eating it. Dogs can't do without meat, but Repin's wife, Natalia Borisovna, didn't eat meat or drink milk, and didn't allow anyone else to have them—not just her guests, but Repin, too, and she fed Mik only porridge of various sorts . . . so in distress he'd gone after the chicken. Now, did he really eat it, and if so, how? Did he tear it to pieces or swallow it whole? This interested Boba and me intensely. And in Repin's studio the pictures weren't really as interesting as the burning question: would our feet show under the thick curtains which covered the canvases if we could play hide-and-seek there? Or: would the coachman let me braid the mane of Repin's horse Lyuba again so the hair wouldn't get in her eyes? And most important of all: was it true what Repin had told me, that a squirrel came up to him every day in the park? I couldn't bring myself to ask, but I was dying to know.

The story went like this: one summer Repin began to paint my portrait. I was walking from the wood across the lawn at Penates one morning (we were allowed to go that way as long as we didn't go too near the house). I was barefoot, boiling hot and all covered with mosquito bites, my hair was uncombed, my teeth all black from blackberries. Suddenly, Ilya Efimovich called to me from the upper balcony. Frightened, I went up to him. Generally, we children weren't shy around him, he was always cordial and somehow attentive to us; we felt his love for Kornei Ivanovich, and also for us; but this time I was frightened—his call seemed so sudden. Maybe I'd stepped on a flower or done something else wrong? But no, he greeted me from above just as warmly as usual, and said from up there: "My, what dappled hair you have . . . Ask your parents if they'd let you come to me at twelve tomorrow, if you're not busy. I'd like to paint you."

The next day, to my astonishment, Kornei Ivanovich himself walked me over to Penates, and the whole way he drummed into me that Repin didn't like to paint children because children can't sit still; that I must sit without wiggling—"once he places you, don't move, not your hands, not your feet, not your shoulders, not your knees."

"But what if a mosquito bites me?" I asked.

"Ignore it," answered Kornei Ivanovich.

Already prepared and waiting for me on the lower balcony were canvas, palette, paints and a stool. At first Ilya Efimovich looked at me with a frown: he was unhappy they'd braided my hair and he unbraided it himself, tousling and tangling it the way it had been the day before, then told me to sit down. I sat down, not knowing where to put my feet, hands, shoulders, fingers, heels, and why humans had so many of them. Repin didn't change my position: "Sit the way you are, only don't turn, and look over here at this bridge." I sat without wiggling; fortunately there weren't any mosquitoes; but something seems to make people want to blink every second. Looking at me, Repin began to dab at the canvas. In order to divert me, he told me that every evening he put a saucer of lemonade on the railing of the bridge and that a squirrel would come down from the pinetrees and lap up the lemonade just the way a kitten laps up milk.

All very well, but unfortunately the sun was on the bridge not the squirrel, and it hurt my eyes to look at it; nonetheless I looked and looked and looked, and when Repin put down his brush and I ran home, colored circles swam in front of my eyes for a long time afterwards.

"Why didn't you tell Ilya Efimovich that your eyes hurt?" asked Kornei Ivanovich.

"People talk with their mouths," I answered pedantically. "What if he'd been drawing my lips just at that moment?"

Repin gave up on my portrait after three sessions. I was delighted: it turned out that sitting without moving was very hard work. But about the squirrel! Did it come or didn't it? Was he telling the truth or making it up?

70

Victor Shklovsky. He lived somewhere not too far away (near the "Dunes" Station, it seems to me) and came to visit sometimes by train, sometimes by sea. He had curly hair, quick eyes, and a quick way of speaking. As soon as he entered a room, he began to argue—not with one person in particular, but with everyone all at once. He spoke loudly and quickly, his words not separate, but somehow stuck together in clumps. I never understood and don't remember what the arguments were about; however, I remember well an adventure which happened to Shklovsky at our place. One day he arrived not by train, but by boat—a dilapidated, gray boat with a dirty white line along the side and splintery oars—and no sooner had he set foot on the beach than he began to argue. He spent the night. Towards evening the next day, when it was time for him to leave, the boat was not there. Victor Borisovich, Kornei Ivanovich, and a whole crowd of us ran along the shore, looking for it among the boats turned upside down on the beach or bobbing up and down at the end of a rope. No. The gray boat with the white line was nowhere to be found. It must have been stolen. We searched along the shore almost a mile and a half in each direction. When we returned, Boba all of a sudden took hold of Victor Borisovich's trousers and began pulling him behind him. He led him along. There at the dock, near a wooden pier, slapping against the light waves, was a beautiful boat, green, with yellow seats and a bright red rudder. It was the old, dilapidated boat. It had been repainted. In the twenty-four hours Victor Borisovich had stayed with us, the paint had dried and begun to shine. But Boba had recognized it all the same.

Victor Borisovich opened his mouth—to argue! But he thought for a moment, looked carefully, then shook Boba's little hand, put the newly restored oars into their oarlocks, jumped into the boat and rowed off.

The crooks didn't get away with their enterprise.

Khlebnikov. In contrast to Shklovsky, he was always silent; and everything about him was unmoving—his face, his glance, his hands. He sat and kept silent. I remember his silence as a kind of activity, as something he did: if someone back then had asked me what Khlebnikov did, I would have answered: he keeps silent. I knew that he was a poet, but I don't remember his reciting; was that because he didn't recite while he was at our house, or because I couldn't listen to his poetry? I don't know. But whatever the reason, it was not his poetry, but his drawings that impressed me. In contrast to their creator, the vivid faces which he drew in black pencil in *Chukokkala* seemed loud. But even these faces were motionless.

I remember the motor yacht that couldn't manage to tie up off our beach —too shallow!—and the sailors in their caps with gold ribbons, and the small boat called a launch which was sent from the yacht, and the man in a white sweater wearing binoculars around his neck about whom I'd heard so much conversation: Leonid Andreev. But I hardly looked at him. I was much more interested in the sailor. His striped vest. His ribbon fluttering in the breeze with the golden letters "Distant." They were my first motor and my first sailor. The sound of the motor, knocking, dead, alien to the splash of the waves, to the blue of the sky and the silence.

I remember the day when Chaliapin, visiting at Penates, came to see Kornei Ivanovich. I didn't get the chance to hear him sing; but when he went upstairs to the study on the second floor, I looked out the window in bewilderment—it seemed as if the trees in the garden were making noise. He was singing to himself as he climbed the stairs. It astounded me that he was not only broader through the shoulders, larger, more enormous than our father, but also a whole head taller. "A papa and a half." The door to the study closed behind them, and his broad-chested dog, wearing a coat with little bells on it, froze there, teeth bared, nose to the door. Not for one moment did she move away from the door behind which her master was hidden. It was the first time I had seen a dog in a coat . . . She was unpleasant looking, hoarse, and breathed loudly through her nose . . . Chaliapin had a Chinese valet—the first Chinese I'd ever seen—wearing a long braid and baggy trousers. He treated me with refined politeness as if I were a grown-up lady, which embarrassed me a great deal; and he gave Kolya some Chinese stamps for his stamp album. Time and again we ran over to the yardman's lodge at Repin's to see him, drawn by his yellow face, braid, trousers, and bows.

The sailor and the motor amazed me most about Andreev; the Chinaman and the dog with his bells, about Chaliapin. The sailor, the motor, and the dog were all firsts for me. True, I was seeing Leonid Andreev and Chaliapin for the first time also, but what was special about them? A writer, an opera singer, in other words, just people, ordinary, commonplace, what we were used to. But a sailor! But a valet, and a Chinese one to boot! Now that was something! As to the world renown of Andreev, Repin or Chaliapin, fortunately, the "air of art" we breathed left us children, did not teach us to stare at famous people. The concept of celebrity was unknown to us. And famous people also knew how to behave as if they were completely unaware of their personal fame.

Kornei Ivanovich was certainly pleased that the presence of Leonid Andreev or Chaliapin did not make us feel as though we were special: "Chaliapin was at our house!" He wanted us to grow up like children anywhere. The charades, the boat, going barefoot, skittles, skiing, and excursions were intended to keep us children. Yet at the same time, as I now understand, given his own enormous appreciation of talent, he was a bit chagrined, almost shocked to learn that because there were so many celebrities at our house we came to see them as ordinary. It erased their miraculousness. We forgot how lucky we were to have them there—something he never forgot. Repin? What's so special about Repin? Korolenko: "Oh, Papa, I forgot," announced Kolya, "Vladimir Galaktionovich came by when you were out . . .

Imagine, he was on a bicycle, leaned his bicycle against the fence and came to talk to us... He asked me to tell you... What do you think, which would be faster: the slowest train or the fastest bicyclist?"

Sometimes it seemed to him as if precious stones were being poured out before our eyes, but we did not see their shine and preferred to play pebble games on the beach with other boys and girls.

All right. At our age it's normal to play with pebbles... But all the same...

He needn't have worried. A few decades later, when I was no longer seven, but thirty, I remember telling him that I was seeing Anna Akhmatova regularly (at one point he had introduced me to her briefly). His response was to demand anxiously:

"I hope you understand that you ought to record every word she says?"

I understood. And I am indebted to him for this understanding, to his relationship with poetry and culture, to his feeling for continuity, to *Chukokkala*, to that morning when I saw the careful way he touched original Nekrasov manuscripts.

Yes, one day he did show Kolya and me Nekrasov manuscripts.

In 1914, after Chukovsky's first Nekrasov publications, Anatoly Fedorovich Koni gave him a phenomenal gift: the originals of *Who is Happy in Russia, Princess Volkonsky,* and some other treasures, both rough drafts and final copies. And one day Kornei Ivanovich solemnly invited Kolya and me to come to his study, took us by the hand and led us up to his desk—just the way one would lead a small child to a lighted Christmas tree. His desk was always tidy after he finished working, but today it was more a pulpit or a shrine than a desk. Not a speck of dust. Books, papers, pencils, glue, inkwell, pens had been moved to the windowsill, and in the middle of the desk an open document case and in it...

I have to confess I don't remember whether what I saw was notebooks or separate sheets of paper. It seems to me separate sheets, but I can't say for sure. They were big, yellowed, written in faded ink. I also don't remember if it was the manuscript for *Princess Volkonsky* or for *Who is Happy in Russia.* But it was a Nekrasov manuscript. And I clearly remember my feelings.

By that time I had already seen plenty of manuscripts, the articles which Kornei Chukovsky wrote, tore up, and wrote again. But everything about this one seemed strange to me: the handwriting, the yellow color, and the extreme care, solemnity and gentleness with which those long, suntanned fingers touched the old, crumpled pages. But strangest of all was the discovery that verses I'd heard recited and read in books had actually been composed and written down first! A discovery? Of course I already knew: "Nekrasov wrote *Who is Happy in Russia,*" but I didn't really understand it until that moment. Kornei Ivanovich named some year—some mythically long ago time, which I instantly forgot; the date was crowded out by the thought that, necessarily, *before* that date, the poem did not exist, had simply never existed, in the same way that Boba, say, had not existed before June 1910. Unlike the sea, the sand and the stars, these verses hadn't always been on earth; a human being, Nikolai Alekseevich Nekrasov, had written them. The same sort of thing as Mayakovsky walking along those stones composing his verses, which only began to exist at that moment.

Nekrasov had written poetry right there on that very paper. Before that, the verses had not existed.

Kolya noticed that one of the sheets was blank. Completely blank, not a line, not a word, not a letter. And it was crumpled. One corner was turned down at the top of the page.

"That one's not necessary," he said, like a boy who has caught the teacher in a mistake. "Look, Papa, nothing's written on that page. You can throw it away."

Turning his whole body to face Kolya, Kornei Ivanovich looked at him with indignant interest. He didn't get angry. He thought for a second how to explain. Then answered very carefully:

"It's blank, that's true, but you see, Nekrasov touched it. Do you understand? He wrote nothing on it, but since the page is there among the others which are written upon, Nekrasov must have touched it, looked at it. Do you understand? It mustn't be torn up or thrown away. It came from that very time, from that age, from the drawer of Nekrasov's desk."

From that age. From that desk. And now it lies here before us on this desk.

I don't know what Kolya understood, but I understood very little. Nekrasov, like everybody else, had hands and touched these sheets of paper with those hands. So what? Why couldn't you throw away a blank, crumpled piece of paper?

That's what I thought, that's the way I looked at it, because the lesson was still a bit hard for me. But some slight glimmer of understanding about the change from decade to decade, about the passage of time, and the links between one age and another was laid down, was established back then—in the light of that clear, sunny, childhood day lying across that old paper.

. . . Yes, Kornei Ivanovich captivated, enticed, educated and sometimes actually played teacher. He preached culture and its creators. For good reason, the following quotation from Carlyle turned up recently in one of his letters to Koni: "There can be no more noble feeling in the breast of a man than admiration for those who are greater than he!"

Sometimes, for lack of patience, he grew indignant and got angry.

The sound of those outbursts is preserved in the child's memory.

He is reciting poetry on the veranda one evening. Not to us but to some adult guests. But we're there, too; we can't be torn away from the sound of his voice.

Beneath the bank and track, in ditch unmown,
As if alive, she lies unblinking,
Around her braids, a colored scarf is thrown;
So young and so good-looking.

. . . .

. . . .

The trains on their accustomed circuit,
Went rattling past, with noisy creaking,
Blue and yellow cars were quiet;
From green, the sound of sobs and singing.[4]

Suddenly, in the midst of this weeping and singing of wagons, roads, and loneliness, in the middle of this grief turned to happiness through harmony, there occurred "...an awkward, ugly, one-of-a-kind interruption..."[5] Nanny Tonya ran onto the veranda and asked, out of breath: "Shall I bring out the samovar? It's boiling."

The evening was cool, and they'd urged her to be quick with the samovar.

Looking at her in astonishment, as if one of them must be crazy, Kornei Ivanovich furiously smashed a dish, cut his finger, and shouted: "How could you—how could you—interrupt poetry?!"

Tonya burst into tears. He had shouted at her not only in the middle of poetry, but in front of guests. This was the same irreproachable fellow who insisted upon politeness to servants from us children as well as from himself, who as a sick old man hesitated to ask a housemaid to bring him a hot water bottle because she'd have to climb the stairs an extra time!... After exploding on the Kuokkala veranda, he quickly came to his senses and hurried to the kitchen to ask Tonya's forgiveness. He comforted her and as he did so carefully explained:

"If someone is reciting poetry, I can think of only one reason to interrupt—if the house is burning down! I can think of no other reason!"

(We were already trained. We'd learned long ago and unmistakably that we mustn't interrupt an out-loud recitation, and sometimes not even a silence. A cold winter's day and you've hauled a pot of soup or tea over to him at someone else's dacha, where he's gone to finish some article or other; he sits there silently, pencil in hand. The silence must not be interrupted. Set the food on the windowsill and leave quickly, without saying a word. If you say something at the wrong time, how he bellows! But if he or someone else should be reciting poetry...)

Once he bellowed at me—for a similar reason—and just as loudly as at Tonya.

...Once again we're on the Big Road, in wintertime, returning from somewhere, just the two of us. It's not really cold, about minus five degrees, no colder. A light snow is falling. No sparkling crust of ice: everything is soft, soft, puffy, soundless, colorless. Nothing sparkles dark blue-white-rose-light blue, it's just white.

We've had to retreat to the snowbank at the side of the road: a string of ice wagons is moving slowly up a side road and past us on the Big Road.

The horses, dusted with snow, move with difficulty in the soft road; Finns walk beside the wagons, wearing jackets, felt boots, quilted trousers stuffed into their boots, and four-cornered fur-lined leather hats—the shining leather makes the hats look like helmets. The line of carts drags by slowly, boringly: I am tired of watching the horses and the opaque rectangles of just-cut ice. Oh look, in one of them, inside, as if in a glass, there's a pine branch! How did it get there, and how can they get it out? Do they smash ice to bits?

At last all the carts creak past. The last horse, the last lump of ice, the last helmet.

We step onto the road. And then a new obstacle—Repin. Turns out he has been on the other side of the road. Wearing warm shoes and a soft fur hat and all covered with snow, he's been waiting like us for the carts to pass.

I'm disappointed: now they'll want to talk. Another delay!

Repin, taking off his glove, politely greets Kornei Ivanovich, then holds out his hand to me.

No, we didn't have to wait long. They decided something about a "Wednesday."

Another polite shaking of hands, and Repin disappears off into the snow. We continue through the snow in one direction, he in the other.

But we haven't gone ten steps when something very strange occurs. My father becomes a demon. Kornei Ivanovich suddenly tears the glove off my hand and throws it as far as he can into a snowbank at the foot of someone else's fence.

"Repin offered you his hand without a glove," he cries in a fury, "and you had the gall to offer yours with the glove on! Good-for-nothing! Whose nose were you waving your mitten under? With that same hand he drew 'They Did Not Expect Him' and 'Mussorgsky.' Dunce!"

Just like Nanny Tonya, I began to wail.

Just like Nanny Tonya, I didn't understand what I'd done wrong. Repin had greeted me. I'd held out my hand and said, "How do you do." How was I to know you shouldn't shake hands with a glove on? No one had told me. And wasn't this the very same, everyday Repin who had told me about the squirrel, and always gave Kolya and me candy when we brought him a note from Papa, and let us run up and down the staircases in his house? Repin, just Repin. What was all this about?

It wasn't fair!

And who was it "they didn't expect"? And who was this "Mussorgsky"?

Kornei Ivanovich's anger was probably wrong and unfair and certainly not pedagogically sound. He would have done much better simply to have explained to me, slowly, cheerfully, half-jokingly, as he could do so well, that when shaking hands with adults children should always take off their glove. After all he had explained to Kolya, once and for all, without any shouting, that a boy crossing the threshold of any house or meeting anyone on the road should take off his cap first thing. Why did he have to shout at me? And then, wading up to his waist in snow to retrieve the glove from the fence, bang me as hard as he could across the shoulders with it, as if to shake off the snow, but really to work off his remaining anger?

Yet how grateful I am to him today for that injustice, for that insult I suffered so unfairly!

For that instructive anger with which he exploded when he thought I did not show enough respect for the hand held out to me by art!

CHAPTER

XI

" . . . the person who has not experienced an intense passion for literature, poetry, music, paintings, who has not passed through this schooling of
the emotions, remains forever an emotional cripple, no matter how great
may be his scientific and technical achievements. The first time I meet
such people, I always notice their frightening defect—their poverty of spirit,
their 'obtuseness of heart' (as Herzen calls it)."

Thus wrote Kornei Ivanovich after a lifetime of experience, in 1965, in an
article entitled "On Spiritual Illiteracy."[1]

Meeting with people of "obtuse heart" aroused in him mixed feelings of
anger, scorn and pity. In the end pity always gained the upper hand.

"Emotional cripples," people who, for lack of emotional schooling, remained "spiritually illiterate," aroused not only his scorn, but also his
compassion. After all, doesn't this "frightening defect," this "poverty of
spirit," deserve every bit as much pity as a physical defect like blindness or
deafness?

He wrote of a girl who was unable in 1965 to enjoy reading Gogol, to
catch the transition from one tonality to another, from quiet smile to belly
laugh, from belly laugh to prophetic pathos, with the kind of compassion
one would feel for a hunchback or a man without legs.

"No one taught her to delight in art, to enjoy Gogol, Lermontov, to make
lifelong companions of Pushkin, Baratynsky, Tyutchev, and *I pitied her as
people pity a cripple.*"*

In his Diary there's yet another term for spiritual cripples: "souls bereft."

The word "poor" figured prominently in his lexicon. It had a special
meaning for him in addition to its generally accepted one.

"Poor, poor silly hen!" wrote Kornei Ivanovich in an article on children's
language. He was writing about a mother who had heaped abuse on him for
daring to suggest that parents should listen carefully to the way children

---

*Italics are the Author's.

speak. Answering the angry matron, he repeated his arguments, citing authoritative, scholarly works, and having mocked the ignorance of his correspondent to his heart's content, exclaimed in conclusion:

"Poor, poor silly hen!"[2]

These words are certainly mocking, but the mockery is muted with compassion. For in its own way hers, too, is a "soul bereft." It is possible to become a thinking, learning, nurturing human being—an honest-to-goodness mother!—but remain a hen, clucking meaninglessly over her hatchling chick... Then several decades later he called a self-assured American lady who had mutilated a book of his in her English translation: "Poor, poor hack-writer!" First, letters full of thunder and lightning both to and about her, but in conclusion: "Poor, poor!"

These words are certainly mocking, but the mockery is muted with compassion. For in its own way hers, too, is a "soul bereft." It is possible to become a thinking, learning, nurturing human being—an honest-to-goodness mother!—but remain a hen, clucking meaninglessly over her hatchling chick... Then several decades later he called a self-assured American lady who had mutilated a book of his in her English translation: "Poor, poor hack-writer!" First, letters full of thunder and lightning both to and about her, but in conclusion: "Poor, poor!"

"A vain and envious scoundrel" is what he called a certain literary type who constantly criticized him from the heights of his erudition and genius. One might think this description said it all. But no: again that "poor;" "I feel sorry for him... Poor devil, poor devil!"

1926. Leningrad. Once more a diary entry. Here the special meaning of the word "poor" becomes absolutely, strikingly, precisely, piercingly clear.

A case of embezzlers at a playing card factory: the trial of Baturlin and others. Over the months they had accumulated tens of thousands of rubles, and until the embezzlement was discovered, lived entirely as they pleased.

Kornei Ivanovich spent a day in the courtroom. When he returned home, he wrote: "These *poor** embezzlers bought nothing except women, wine, restaurants and similar boredom. But women can be got for free, especially by such young and pretty men—and wine? Wouldn't going to the Hermitage provide greater pleasure? Is it possible that *no one ever told them* that reading Fet, for instance, is sweeter than any wine? Not long ago Dobychin was visiting me, and I began to recite line after line of Fet, I just couldn't stop. I chose all my favorites, and it was such bliss I thought my heart would burst —*I can't imagine that there are people for whom this is actually dead and unnecessary.* It seems only in commemorative articles we say Fet's poetry is 'one of the highest achievements of Russian lyric poetry,' but almost no one knows that lyric poetry can *fill a man with happiness* from head to toe

---

*Author's italics throughout.

—Baturlin didn't know this, Ivanov didn't know this. Entin, the judges, and the prosecutor don't know this either."

That's why they were "poor." To them, everything he lived for was "dead and unnecessary." They had never experienced the sort of "happiness which can fill a man from head to toe," the "bliss" from which "the heart" might "burst."

The judges also were "poor"—for the very same reason.

He believed that art could not only forge a new soul, not only endow a person with happiness, it could also renew the physical self.

"...what would be wonderful for us both," he wrote in the thirties to S. Ya. Marshak, "would be to go somewhere near a warm ocean, take Blake and Whitman with us and read them under the open sky. What is common to us both is that poetry gives us the deepest—an almost unearthly—kind of *refreshment* and immediately renews our physical being. Do you remember how in the midst of 'Rainbow'* squabbles and annoyances we could read Tyutchev or Shevchenko to the point of tears and clear our heads? I have never read poetry with anyone as *purifyingly* as I did with you."

Poor, poor embezzlers! This way of purifying their souls and renewing themselves physically was unknown to them. His pity for the emotionally and intellectually deprived was sincere. He always remembered them, could not forget about them, because when he came into contact with them he experienced immediate, spontaneous pain. It was as if he lived for others subjunctively: he saw clearly what a person *could* but had not become. He believed that the happiness bestowed by art was contagious, that this happiness could and should be shared with other people, that it could make the lame to walk, and the blind to see. He was always teaching someone—reading and writing, English—or choosing books for someone. He believed in the omnipotence of literature as others believe in the omnipotence of religion. At one point (in the middle of the twenties, during NEP**) observing some passersby who astonished him by the vulgarity of their behavior, speech, clothing, faces, he poured out his sorrow in a letter, which he concluded with the following words of hope:

"...then suddenly the quiet word 'book' came to mind. The word is voiceless, like the letters 'b' and 'k'..." These people "don't know yet that they have Pushkin and Blok. This opium still lies before them. Oh, how their gait would change, their profile be ennobled, and the intonation of their speech be altered if these people should come across Chekhov, for instance... Doesn't the very color of a person's eye and shape of his lip change after he has read *War and Peace?* Books regenerate the very organism of a man, change his blood, his appearance—return ten years from now to

---

*From the name of the publishing house: Rainbow. (Author)
**Lenin's New Economic Policy. (Translator)

Zagorodny Prospect and what a lot of wonderful, contemplative, truly human faces you will see."[3]

More than once he quoted Dostoevsky's similarly hopeful words: "...and do you know that sometimes in the general mood of life a certain idea, concern or sorrow, accessible only to the person of high education and developed intellect, can suddenly be conveyed to the virtually illiterate, crude creature who has never cared about anything, and infect his soul with its influence?"[4]

All Kornei Ivanovich's work—as portraitist, critic, literary historian, storyteller, translation theorist; all his work in every genre—feuilleton, textual study, research—was always contagious, "infected with its own influence." Whether he was ridiculing banal novels, seeking the key to the creativity of Korolenko or the poetic individuality of Anna Akhmatova or Alexander Blok, or commenting on newly discovered lines of Nekrasov, he injected the bracing drug of his passion for art into the blood of his reader as if through a sharp needle. His articles on literature were full of stormy emotion and unexpected ideas. And they were always addressed to two audiences at once: "to the person of great education and developed intellect" and to the "crude" creature "who has never cared about anything." To those who rubbed elbows at Repin's Penates, at art exhibit openings, on the editorial boards of literary journals, at premieres in the Art Theater or in the theaters of Komissarzhevskaya and Meyerhold, at debates in the auditorium of the Tenishev School and at Vyacheslav Ivanov's "tower"—and also to the provincial, unsophisticated, "crude" folk for whom he delivered his lectures in Vilnius, earlier in Odessa, or in squalid halls in Zhitomir, Bialystok, Uman. Agree with him or no: the drug of passion for art transfused their blood. The audiences were different: in Petersburg or Kuokkala they were cultured, in Bialystok, ignorant, but the result was the same. He said of himself in those years that he was "always a street," "a shout," that he wrote for the "gallery." Why did they print his articles in Bryusov's highbrow magazine *The Scales*, why did Repin, Rozanov, Remizov, Korolenko, and Koni find his articles interesting? And the futurists, acmeists, and symbolists! I remember when Yevgeny Victorovich Tarle at the end of the thirties recited to me *by heart* whole pages he liked from articles by the young Chukovsky—Tarle, the distinguished author of scholarly works on Russian and world history. What sort of "gallery" is an academician! But Chukovsky was, indeed, read by "the gallery" and "the tower," and his particular talent was that he could raise the street to the tower, not bring the tower down to the street. A popularizer? No, a popularizer presents someone else's ideas in simplified form. Popularization didn't interest Koni, Tarle or Repin. Chukovsky always offered his own ideas, some so new and unexpected that he shocked many with the paradoxical nature of his methods and conclusions. He said of himself: "I can write only *by invention*; I could not set forth someone else's ideas."

"I only enjoy writing when I feel I am revealing something new, some-

Kornei Chukovsky with Boba, Lydia, and Kolya on the seashore, 1912 or 1913 (?)

Lydia, Ilya Repin, Kornei Chukovsky, Maria Borisovna, Natalia Borisovna Nordman-Severova (Repin's wife), and Kolya

The Chukovsky dacha at Kuokkala

Lydia with Kornei Chukovsky, 1911

Lydia and Kolya with Kornei Chukovsky's mother, Ekaterina Osipovna Korneichukova

Kornei, Lydia, Maria Borisovna, and Kolya

Kornei Chukovsky windsailing on the Gulf of Finland with children and friend

The Chukovsky family at dinner

Kornei Chukovsky with Kolya, Boba, and Lydia, 1913 (?)

Kornei Chukovsky at his desk

thing no one else has said. That's, of course, an illusion, but as long as it lasts I'm happy." He attracted both "the tower" and "the street" with the novelty of his "inventions." One of the secrets of his writing which deserves study and explanation is its simultaneous focus on two audiences, his invariable awareness of "bereft souls."

From the debate platform and the newspaper page he generally achieved victory, succeeded in exciting, inciting, and inspiring. But when he ran into psychological ugliness in real life, he often suffered defeat.

In Kuokkala, as a girl of eight, I once saw his helpless anger turn in a moment into helpless pity, or more accurately, absolute despair.

It went according to that same pattern: "Scoundrel! Poor, poor wretch."

This time there were two scoundrels. Children: two hooligans aged thirteen or fourteen.

One hot July day we walked to the train station together to meet Mama. We left too early and arrived at the station platform forty minutes before the train. Kornei Ivanovich couldn't stand wasting time away from work, and vexed by his miscalculation, he crossed the tracks, jumped down from the platform onto the coarse sand, blackened with soot from the locomotive, hunched himself next to a stump on the embankment and began to write, resting his paper on the stump. (He loved to write away from his desk, to set himself up with a board or a book wherever he happened to be —in bed, on a stump, on a window sill, on a rock by the sea.) I stretched out a short distance away, lazily picking out my favorite parts of *Oliver Twist* in Vvedensky's translation—a book I knew almost by heart—not so much reading, as marveling at the way the grains of sand scattered on the page grew into boulders when I screwed up my eyes. I screwed up my eyes, shook off the sand, then screwed them up again.

Up above us where the embankment ended and the woods began, two boys were lighting a fire. Raising his head from his stump, Kornei Ivanovich had already caught sight of them. He loved campfires, was a master at lighting them, and jumped over flames so high my heart would sink into my boots. Any minute I expected him to leave his work, stand up and approach the fire. But the boys began to smoke and then to cough, and he turned away in disgust. The sight of children smoking always repelled him. (He himself never smoked and never drank, and all his life expressed utter amazement that anyone could actually take pleasure from these activities.) The boys stamped out their fire, spat a couple of times, and threw away the butts. (Defiling the woods with the butts! That also always disgusted him.) Then the boys invented a new amusement for themselves. They climbed down onto the track, and jumping face-to-face, together and back across the rails, began trying to outshout each other with obscenities.

Kornei Ivanovich jumped up, thrust his pencil and paper into my hands, and with three steps came up beside the boys.

"What are you doing?" he shouted. "Shut up at once!"

Impudently staring at him, they went right on.

He grabbed first one then the other by the collar and threw them down on the packed sand.

They crawled away, then stood up, looking at him apprehensively now, not challengingly—was he going to beat them?—shook themselves off and ran up the slope. Then from the higher ground among the pine trees, feeling themselves safe, they thumbed their noses, danced about and began shouting obscenities all over again.

He set off up the hill after them. He wouldn't have been able to catch both of them, but with his long arms he could probably have grabbed at least one. He rushed up the hill, and black streams of sand showered down on me from under his huge feet.

"Swine!" he shouted. ("Mediocrity" and "swine" were the strongest swearwords he ever used.) "I'll show you..."

Then suddenly, halfway up, he stopped. He stood motionless, head down, as if staring at the sand, not taking a step either up or down toward me. The boys pirouetted triumphantly, and one even felt brave enough to chuck a pine cone at him.

"Poor things, you poor, poor things!" Kornei Ivanovich cried out suddenly in that heartrending, anguished voice with which he recited particularly favorite poems. He sobbed, "You've been robbed. No one ever told you anything, you've never heard anything except those vile words..."

He gave up and climbed back down. Tears were rolling down his cheeks. Much upset, I took his hand. I don't know whether I would have found something to say to him if we had not at that moment heard an approaching roar.

"Papa, the train!" I shouted, and scooping up book, pencil, and paper, we ran for the platform.

CHAPTER
XII

I learned to read uncommonly early. This chance circumstance played a large role in my life and a not unimportant role in the Kuokkala part of my father's life.

Not only did he read to us in Kuokkala, I also read to him. Regularly, every evening. Unless I read to him, he couldn't fall asleep.

Kornei Ivanovich, healthy giant, swimmer, and skier, from early childhood to his dying day suffered from an incurable disease—insomnia. It was the price he paid for his heightened impressionability, his obsession with work. Lying down to sleep, he could put out his candle for the night, but not put his work out of his mind. In the carefully guarded, total silence of the house, in the drawn-curtain darkness, the spinning wheel of his thoughts would continue to whirl. It had no brakes. Having tossed vainly for two hours, he would give in to his insomnia—and his work. The illness often turned a full day of work into a round-the-clock stint. "I sit at my desk, not knowing if it's night or day" (a line from a letter). At night he usually didn't sit at his desk but worked lying down: he'd set his candle in its candlestick in the corner of the sofa, a board and piece of paper on his pointy raised knees. In the evening, when he went to bed, the knowledge that he'd not finished an article would keep him from falling asleep—beginnings, endings, transitions, examples, contradictions, revelations roiling in his brain would drive him to jump up and grab his pen; then in the morning, when the article seemed finished (though not for long!), he'd be too tired to sleep. He'd come downstairs looking emaciated, older, overgrown with black bristle, responding to nothing at all, limp and irritable at the same time.

Life for the whole house was determined by the morning bulletin: "Papa slept," "Papa didn't sleep." It meant two different houses, two different papas.

His only hope of falling asleep lay in reading. Not his own, someone else's. He needed someone to read out loud to him at night. A soothing, even voice. And a book which would take him a thousand miles from the thoughts he'd been thinking all day. The book had to be interesting—a boring one wouldn't do!—but not too interesting, because a new interest would also excite him and keep him from falling asleep. The best sort of book for putting him to sleep was one he'd already read and loved but half forgotten. Then it was pleasant to listen to but not too exciting. For the reader, however, the book had to be new and irresistibly fascinating. Otherwise, he'd get bored and sleepy . . . and then . . . then human charity would require urging the reader to leave and letting insomnia have its way. "Go, go, it's time for you to go to bed" (the desperate prayer: "stay!").

It was necessary to read smoothly, without too much expression, in a calming, lullaby-like way, but at the same time with obvious interest. The intrusion of another world—the feelings, thoughts, and images of other people—forcibly distracted him from the latest cause of his madness: from the latest article storming the author's brain, try as he might to forget it . . . It was necessary to erect a bar, a barrier with another's text.

No bromide, no mixture of Bekhterev's, not even a meeting with Dr. Bekhterev himself, not the hypnotist whom Repin specially invited to meet with him, not physical labor, not fresh air—nothing gave him relief from his illness.

What relieved him was to go to bed as early as possible and listen to someone read. In Leningrad, Moscow, Peredelkino, he went to bed at nine ⟋ or ten o'clock, in Kuokkala—at eight, along with little Boba. Suffering from insomnia and trying to gain relief from it, this twenty-five-year-old man, young, sociable, thirsty for anything new, chopped out of his day, once and for all, its most social time—the evening, and together with the evening, the fascinating, noisy, varied excitement of city life: theaters, debates, jubilees, discussions until dawn, island excursions, restaurants. (He did take part in these affairs, in premieres and jubilees, but only on very rare occasions . . . Once, in Petrograd, after four tortured hours of trying vainly to fall asleep, he got up, dressed, and sorrowfully went off to a party, the birthday of Ekaterina Pavlovna Letkova-Sultanova. The guests, flabbergasted to see him at half-past one in the morning, didn't believe their eyes. "Chukovsky, go home to bed, for God's sake. Seeing you at such an hour is wild, unnatural and terrifying," wrote Alexei Tolstoy in *Chukokkala*.)

All his life Kornei Ivanovich paid doubly, triply in cruel insomnia for every train trip (noise and people), for every night spent with friends, even the most hospitable and affectionate (bedtime was not eight o'clock), for every hotel visit (voices, footsteps in the corridor, no one to read to him).

All his life at our house, in Kuokkala, in Leningrad, in Moscow, in Peredelkino, "we read to Papa," then later, when we children grew up and like our children, his grandchildren, began to call him Grandpa—"read to Grandpa." All his life when he was at home, his children, grandchildren, secretaries, relatives, friends, acquaintances read to him; in the hospital or at a sanatorium, if no close friend or relative came specially for that purpose, then neighbors on the corridor or nurses would do it.

In the early twenties in Petrograd, Kolya composed some funny verses about a time we couldn't possibly imagine: a time when our noisy, strong, mischievous father would be old and even Boba (he was then twelve, though just recently in Kuokkala he'd been little), our Boba also would be an old man:

> Then he said, Kornei Ivanich,
> Won't you read me to sleep, Bobich!
> Boba now is bent with age:
> Without his specs can't read a page.

We laughed until we cried. Boba, tall, green-eyed, broad-shouldered, black-browed and pale-skinned, with eyelashes halfway down his cheeks— Boba an old man! And needing, for some unknown reason, some kind of spectacles! Oh, such foolishness could only occur in rhymes! (In fact, Boba never did have a chance to grow old, didn't live long enough to need an old man's spectacles: in the fall of 1941, at the age of 32, he was killed outside Mozhaisk, not far from the Borodino battlefield, as he was returning from reconnaissance duty.)

Although not as an old man, he did manage to read Papa a few books. (He also managed to become a hydrological engineer, to marry, to work on the Niva-stroy Project and the Chirchik Canal and to join up as a soldier with a volunteer militia unit.)

Boba often read to Papa in Petrograd, and sometimes in Moscow.

In Kuokkala, almost every evening, it was I who read. Every evening from eight until ten, until eleven, until I was hoarse, until there were spots in front of my eyes, until he was breathing evenly and sleeping soundly, or until he waved his long hand despairingly: "Enough, Lidochka, enough. It's time for you to go to bed. I can't get to sleep anyway." The long hand drops feebly beside the long body; he lies on his side, back to the wall, as if mortally wounded, the embodiment of despair.

In the morning, before my brothers, I was the first to run to his study on reconnaissance: had he or had he not slept? How well I remember that worn-out pillow, turned a hundred times from one side to the other, those pitiable, wax-spotted pages of manuscript, the books spread out all over the floor, the rumpled, tortured blanket, the twisted sheets hanging down to the floor. It was as if a swarm of demons or a gang of robbers had spent the night there. "No, Lidochka, I didn't sleep at all. You put me to sleep, but I woke up the minute you left."

So it was my fault! I should have read longer! An hour, two hours. I had checked, had stopped reading both in the room and outside the door. He'd been asleep. But apparently I'd been wrong to trust his sleep—in the same way one can sometimes wrongly trust ice near the shore, when, in fact, the ice only appears to be firm. I should have stayed and read longer. My heart ached with repentance and pity.

By the second half of his life, between the ages of fifty and sixty, his illness began to ease a little. A kind of compensation set in, as sometimes occurs with those who suffer from heart disease. In Peredelkino, if he had not slept during the night, then in the morning after breakfast he would without fail fall asleep for an hour and a half; or suddenly, in the middle of the day, at a most unexpected moment, there'd appear tacked to his study door a sign pencilled in large black letters: I AM SLEEPING!!!—with three exclamation points; he had, in his words, all of a sudden "given out," and having taken a daytime nap, he got up refreshed...

Our Kuokkala period coincided with the most vicious period of the ailment. Rarely was he able to nap during the day in Kuokkala, even after two totally sleepless nights. But if it should happen! How the entire household kept watch over his sleep: not only Mama, Nanny Tonya, Kolya, and I, but also little Boba. How fearfully we'd glance at each other at the far-off barking of dogs: they might wake Papa. We guarded the house from both seaside and gateside: from the baker, from the knife sharpener, from "smelts, fresh smelts!", from the chance arrival of a guest.

One day, when Mama had gone to the station leaving us home alone, an unknown gentleman from Petersburg appeared on pressing business just after Kornei Ivanovich had chanced to fall asleep.

Kolya was on guard at the gate.

"Is Kornei Ivanovich at home?" the man asked loudly.

Boba and I came running to help.

"He's home," answered Boba in a whisper.

The newcomer held out his visiting card. Kolya turned it over in his hands.

"Papa's asleep," he said.

"Then go wake him up!" the gentleman exclaimed loudly. "My train leaves in an hour."

"We mustn't wake Papa," I said.

"Aren't there any adults here? I've come on urgent business."

"Nobody wakes up Papa!" said Kolya. "Mama wouldn't either."

Boba, who didn't even come up to the gentleman's waist, quietly tugged him toward the gate.

Shrugging his shoulders, the gentleman turned on his heel and walked away... How was he to know what "Papa's fallen asleep" meant to us and how inconceivable were the words: "Wake Papa up"?

"Idiot!" said Kolya, in the direction of the absolutely blameless guest, and carefully folding the visiting card, tore it to pieces. He didn't even read the last name, so Kornei Ivanovich never found out who it was who'd come to see him on important business. The gentleman was to remain offended forever.

Wake up father. That was a crime! A sacrilege!

In March 1922 Kornei Ivanovich wrote in his diary: "Insomnia poisoned my whole life, because of it I spent my best years—between the ages of twenty-five and thirty-five—as an invalid..."

The period when he was most sharply conscious of himself as an invalid, when his insomnia was at its most insomniac, that period was Kuokkala, my childhood.

Actually, he was never entirely free from serious bouts of his illness.

Never, even when sleeping pills, which he called "putting-to-sleepers," became available—a large, round metal box labeled "sleeps" stood near his ottoman in Peredelkino with a whole pile of these drugs, domestic and foreign, but the "sleeps" didn't guarantee him sound repose. He still required, in addition to a sleeping pill, his old reliable remedy, someone reading out loud to him.

People took turns reading to him: Marina Nikolaevna, Kolya's wife; Klara Israelevna, his longtime secretary; his children and grandchildren. Chance guests.

References to his insomnia in his diary and his letters read like *Diary of a Madman*: "Mother, save your poor son!"

"My insomnia has gone beyond bounds. Not only can I not sleep, I can't even lie down; I ran around my room *howling* for hours" (1946).

Howling... Now if that's not madness?

"You lay your head on the pillow, and begin to doze off, but not quite all the way, just a little bit more—and you'll lose consciousness completely, but it's just that little bit which you need. Awareness grows keener: 'Am I sleeping or not? will I fall asleep, or not?' you spy on just that little bit, is it increasing or decreasing, and because of that spying you end up not sleeping at all. Today it got so bad I beat myself over the head with my fists! Beat my idiotic skull 'til it was black and blue, if only I could exchange it—oh! oh! oh!" (1924)

Beat himself over the head... Now, if that's not madness?

His book "wrote itself like a novel, but after a few chapters I fell ill with insomnia and now I can't write another line. I sit at my desk day after day and laboriously produce nothing but trash" (1919).

"I've forgotten the meaning of sleep here: there's no one to read to me. If I'd found a reader, I could have slept every night: the main thing is to divert my thoughts from work" (1951).

By chance, the person who read to him most to divert his thoughts from his work, when I was between six and ten, was I. Our mama, Maria Borisovna, was too nervous a woman to calm his agitation. Kolya could not hide his yawns, and Kornei Ivanovich would soon send him off to bed. I not only loved reading out loud, but was ready to appear wide awake the whole night through if it would let him sleep. This also was a game, and what a game: first, it was just between him and me, no one else; secondly, it wasn't really a game, but the most important of all jobs—I was putting Papa to sleep!; and thirdly, I was his commander, not he mine. I was putting my own father to bed, the way other little girls put their dolls to bed. I played "doll-mother" with him, and not only that, he listened when I gave him orders. That was very flattering.

As if in anticipation of my important future assignment—to lull father to sleep!—I learned to read, as I've said, very early. Kornei Ivanovich began to teach Kolya when he was seven. And I, aged four, hung around. When Kolya learned to read words, Kornei Ivanovich bought us Chekhov's *Kashtanka* in the A.F. Marks edition—a big, square book with pictures and very clear black letters on very white paper. It was too old for both of us, and he really retold it for us rather than read it. Every so often, he'd read us small sections of the text, and give Kolya the chance to read a little bit himself. This for some reason was not at the dacha, but in Petersburg; I don't know why or when—but I can clearly remember the cabmen, the clatter of hooves outside the window, the sound of passing voices, and in Kornei Ivanovich's study on the wall between the windows, four Walt Whitmans all in a row—first as a young man; then older, in a floppy hat; then with a beard; and finally in his old age. I remember a playful kitten called Oscar Wilde, named for an article Kornei Ivanovich wrote about the famous English writer. I had been very ill with something for a long time. At the very height of the illness—and of the Kashtanka story—Kornei Ivanovich went away to lecture in several cities—for a week or two? for ten days? I can't remember. When he left, Chekhov's Kashtanka could already jump on her back legs, howl in time to music, and shoot a pistol. He went away. I began to get better. I was no longer flat on my back, but able to sit up when a telegram from him arrived: he was coming home.

There's his ring at the door. Mama runs to open it. Though I can't see him, I can hear each one of his movements: he's taking off his galoshes, hanging up his coat, coming straight up to me. He sits down on the very edge of the bed, long and folded up. His sharp knees stick out. I'm wearing warm socks and a warm sweater and have a compress round my neck. But I'm no longer feverish. He tells me that Mama has written him that I'll soon be able to get up, that I'm almost well.

On my bed, on top of the blanket, lies *Kashtanka*. He leafs through it distractedly. He asks if Kolya and I have quarreled in his absence, promises to take us both to the circus when I get well.

To the circus! That's where the man in the fur coat took Kashtanka. There she met her real owners.

"What's new with you?" asks Kornei Ivanovich, looking at me: have I grown or not, perhaps lost weight? And with a long finger he tucks a piece of cotton back under the bandage around my neck.

New? My news is that I have begun to read. All by myself I read Kolya *Kashtanka* out loud.

That's my most important news: while he was off traveling wherever he went, I taught myself to read, and all by myself, with my own eyes, read the terrible news in that fat, square book: the goose, Ivan Ivanich, died!

"His master took a dish, poured some water into it from the washstand and went out again to the goose.

'Drink, Ivan Ivanich!' he said gently, setting the dish down before him. 'Drink, my dear.'

But Ivan Ivanich didn't move or open his eyes. His master bent his head toward the dish and dipped his beak into the water, but the goose didn't drink, he opened his wings wider but his head remained lying in the dish.

'No, there's nothing more to do!' sighed the master. 'It's all over. Ivan Ivanich is dead!... Dear creature, my good companion, you are no more! How will I get along without you?'"

I can remember that I was shattered not just by the death of the dear goose, but also by the fact that the words "it's all over" were printed no differently from any of the others in the book, not in much bigger letters or perhaps red letters, but exactly the same way as all the other words. "It's all over"—the goose was dead, and there was the same white paper, the same even black letters.

But he is silent, he doesn't cry out, just quietly turns the pages and tucks the covers around my legs as if nothing has happened.

"But Papa, the goose died, the goose is dead!" I repeat, tears running down my face.

*   *   *   *

Now the scene is no longer our city apartment on Suvorovsky Prospect, Number 40-A, near the Tavrichesky Garden, where I learned to read, or the Annenkov dacha in Kuokkala, where we lived a few years I hardly remember (I vaguely recall that we were robbed there, and that Mama returned there from the hospital with newborn Boba); we are at our dacha on the seashore, catercorner to Repin, which I remember clearly: the sea, the pines, Mama, Papa, our grandmother who visited regularly, my brothers, the rooms and the brook.

Every evening I read to Papa. The activity for him is therapeutic, to distract him from his work so he can sleep; for me, it is literary and educational: for reading aloud he gives me only those books which will be interesting and appropriate for a reader of my age.

1913–17. Pre-revolutionary children's literature bore no relation to art: this concept became a widely accepted truism only in our era, and Kornei Ivanovich's articles, both before and after the revolution, did much to promote it.

So what did I read between the ages of six and ten? What sort of books did he choose for me and Kolya; what did he reluctantly permit, what did he slip into our hands?

It is important to recall them, for the books he gave us reflect his taste, his ideas about literature for children and about poetic education.

In a boat, on seagoing excursions, at the teatable, on the road to the station, he didn't plan his recitations for a specific age—Boba's, mine, or Kolya's. In his last article, he said that from childhood he was accustomed to swimming in "an ocean of poetry,"[1] and he carried us along with him, concerned only that from our earliest years we should know and love the depth, immensity, and boundlessness of poetry.

The books which we read to ourselves or out loud to him were a different matter.

Here it was not a question of an ocean or an immensity, here he was very interested in the correlation between the author and his reader, between a book and a person's age. A child of such-and-such an age should like such-and-such a book. The shoes should fit—but where was one to find them? We had read Pushkin's *Fairy Tales* and also Ershov's *The Little Hunchback Horse*... What else was there for a reader between six and ten?

"Shoes which fit" at that time were shaped and sewn in numbers one could easily count: two or three poems of Sasha Cherny, Maria Moravskaya, Poliksena Solovyova, Natan Vengrov. Blok's poems for children were splendid, but not for children. Some years remained before the appearance of Kornei Ivanovich's *Crocodile*.

One reason the children's books he wrote later gained such general recognition was that the shoes were always made exactly to measure. Each book was written for children of a specific age.

Certainly, age is a relative concept in both a physical and psychological sense. Infants do not all learn to hold up their heads or to sit up in the same month, children do not all cut their first teeth or lose them at the same time, they don't all learn to walk, and then to read at the same time.

Much depends on social environment, climate, heredity.

Nonetheless the concept of age has meaning.

The auditorium is full of children. Chukovsky is reading one of his stories in verse. There is an explosion of laughter—a general one!—always at the same place. Attention, pensiveness, fright. A sigh of relief—a general one. Always at the same place. But what if it should be a general yawn? What if they should start to whisper? For the author that would be a disastrous sign.

A new auditorium. Again hundreds of children of the same age. And again at the same two verses, indifference, yawns, whispers.

As a professional children's writer, appearing before hundreds and thousands of children on the most varied of stages, meeting with them in schools, hospitals, sanatoriums, kindergartens and libraries, reading them his own and others' works, Chukovsky established very accurate age brackets for the understanding of literature, as is evident in his book *From Two to*

Five and his article "Literature for Children." But in the early, pre-*Crocodile* period, when the number of children he could watch was limited to the little ones swarming on the Kuokkala beach and to his own children, he thought about perception, watching different ages, trying above all to understand what children find boring and what interesting. "Boring/not-boring" was one of his basic criteria. Not the only criterion, of course. (Are there not plenty of books with sharply turned plots, which are "entertaining" but soulless, untalented, uninspiring, which with their lack of inspiration stifle understanding of life? And stifle the growth of the soul? Not only do they not teach an understanding of art—they drive people away from it.)

"Boring/not-boring" is not the only criterion, but it is a vital one.

Age is a stairway. Each age-determined step should have its own corresponding art. Kornei Ivanovich dreamed of creating a staircase which would lead the maturing human being to *Eugene Onegin.*

What and in what order should the growing person read, from what to what climb the steps (by himself and with the help of adults) so that by the time he is fourteen, fifteen, or sixteen the stanzas of *Eugene Onegin* will not be too hard for him, will not scare him, but delight him? So that from stair to stair, imbued with deeper meaning, his understanding of Tatiana, of Onegin, of life in the country and in Moscow at that time, of the artistry of Pushkin, of Russian history and Russian poetry will grow? What is it necessary to give the growing child, and in what form and sequence, to shield him from banality which always, in every age, inevitably and ineradicably creeps in through the cracks? What can you give the growing child so he will freely and happily ascend the stair of literary culture, without which there is no spiritual culture? There is no end to this staircase, but what should be its first and its subsequent steps? On behalf of poetry and literature Kornei Ivanovich envied music; it seemed to him that in the study of music, in musical pedagogy, such a stairway had already been built. The road to Beethoven was already laid down. In poetry, in the study of literature, he asserted, the stairway to the top—to Pushkin—was not yet built ... Yet Russian poetry was one of the most powerful kingdoms in the world of poetry. What would happen if the heirs were not able to receive their inheritance?

That danger seemed to him very real.

During his life he worked on every step of that imaginary staircase (he translated, wrote, compiled, edited, and reviewed books for children of different ages), but he devoted special care to the very first steps and stairs.

(His conscious intent was akin to the unconscious aims of simpler folk: what a great number of cradle songs and postcradle songs the common people have created! Far more folk songs, jingles, and counting songs have been created in villages and hamlets for the very youngest children than for older ones. And for good reason. The mastering of one's native language and native poetry happens simultaneously, and further, in one's very earliest years.)

93

In my own time I watched large numbers of mamas and aunties bringing Kornei Ivanovich a much-adored Petya or Ninochka to show him a great marvel: can you imagine it, Petya's only three years and one month old, yet he already knows *Scrub-n-Rub* by heart!

"Petya, this is the very same Chukovsky who wrote *The Boldly Buzzing Fly*, do you understand? Petya, don't be stubborn, don't upset your Mama, recite *Scrub-n-Rub* for Uncle Kornei... Honestly, Kornei Ivanovich, he knows all your little books by heart..."

And Kornei Ivanovich, who had just lightheartedly hopped from the porch to the gate with Petya to see who was fastest, asked him riddles in the hall and curiously watched this new example of the three-year-old, completely forgetting that he was that "same Chukovsky," would droop, but not wanting to insult this latest mama, he'd sit himself obediently on the bench and, slyly half-closing his eyes, listen to Petya—can you believe it! by heart!—recite *Scrub-n-Rub*.

Through all this, he would wonder not at Petya but at Mama.

Upon her departure, he'd sigh and say: "Un-be-liev-a-ble! It has never occurred to her that children develop according to certain stages. Her Petya is not alone, there are a million three-year-old Petyas. He's no more talented than the rest! All these Petyas for some reason learn *Scrub-n-Rub* by heart between three and five. She might wonder why. But she sees only her own Petya, alone in all the world, and imagines him a child prodigy. Yet if a two-year-old after many hearings can't remember both Russian and foreign nursery rhymes like 'What a very bonny mat has the little kittycat' or 'Humpty-Dumpty Sat on a Wall,' and at three or four, *Scrub-n-Rub*, *Fire*, *The Boldly Buzzing Fly*, *The Mail* or *The Absentminded Gentleman*— then he ought to be taken off quickly to the psychiatrist... *Crocodile* is a novel for children from six to eight, and *Scrub-n-Rub* a storylet for three year olds. But she has eyes only for her Petya, others hold no interest for her whatsoever, that's how she can think her Petya a genius. She cannot guess that he is not the exception among children his age, but the rule."

In his article "Literature and School" Kornei Ivanovich writes about the climb up the last steps of the imaginary staircase. He criticizes schools for inadequate attention to age, for their inability to bridge the gap between a twelve-year-old's perceptions and literature. Schoolchildren don't read poetry for pleasure, they only cram for the sake of a good mark. Furthermore, "literature is not the multiplication tables: one must love poetry, not cram it into one's head."[2] The textbook should, for instance, begin its discussion of Pushkin with poems which can kindle children's excitement, but instead children are forced to read early, archaic, abstract Pushkin poems, which frighten them away with their slow movement and complexity. Initially, the textbook should not obey the chronology of Pushkin's work, but the chronology of a child's perceptual ability.

"It is an act of savage hatred for both Pushkin and our children," wrote Chukovsky, "to present a twelve-year-old schoolchild...with an archaic text, full of slavonicisms and incomprehensible metaphors." (He quoted: "I am here, freed from vain fetters, I am learning to find true felicity, to worship the law with a free spirit, to disregard the muttering of the unenlightened masses," etc.) Certainly, he continued, by cramming doggedly they can memorize this text, "but don't ask them to take any joy in the thought of Pushkin."

He inspired that much-to-be-desired joy in Kolya and me by introducing us to Pushkin with "The Lay of Wise Oleg," "The Hussar," "The Bridegroom," and excerpts from "Poltava" and "The Bronze Horseman."

How we delighted in the lines:

> To the oven—right! left! right!... [3]

or:

> How naughty little Mary mine... [4]

or:

> "And from whose finger is this ring?"
> All sudden cried the bride then... [5]

or:

> I love, oh great and martial city,
> The smoke and thunder of your keep... [6]

(Children also love smoke and thunder...)
How proud we were of the Montenegrans who bravely and cleverly sent Bonaparte packing:

> Since that time all native Frenchmen
> Surely hate our land so free,
> And they redden if our cap then
> Without warning they should see. [7]

These lines were not only superb Pushkin poetry, they were also fun and interesting to read, satisfying our thirst at that age for travel, events, emotional excitement.

"Narkompros* stubbornly hides from them the Pushkin they could love," wrote Chukovsky in the article "Literature and School," after a great

---

*The Ministry of Education. (Translator)

deal of experience based on his own and others' children. "It even foists 'Dubrovsky' and 'Winter Morning' on eleven-year-old children (in the fifth grade), that is, once again works which do not correspond at all to their age and interests.

"They would be in love with Pushkin all their lives, if they were given, for instance, 'Delibash':

> The delibash is on a pike,
> The cossack's lost his head!

"But it seems Narkompros does not want to instill in children a love of literature. Let them slave away at the curriculum—with no emotion whatsoever! Take, for example, the fables of Krylov. They have everything children could want: vibrant poetry, amusing stories, and bears, and elephants, and monkeys. Eleven-year-olds are as drawn to these fables as to honey. That's probably why the curriculum includes only three fables, in other words, almost none at all! Don't let them be spoiled by poems which actually give them pleasure! Of all Lermontov's work the one children love best is 'The Song of the Merchant Kalashnikov,'—and, naturally, Narkompros does not include this poem even on their list for outside reading. The same is true for Tolstoy's *Childhood*. And children so love to read about children! Those who compiled the school curriculum simply wouldn't make any allowances for children, and that's that.

"In sum, if the compilers of the curriculum purposely tried to offer children our literature in its most unpalatable, indigestible, and unattractive form, they have succeeded brilliantly."[8]

What did he consider "digestible," "palatable" for me at eight and Kolya at eleven? What did he order, buy, and slip into our hands in Kuokkala?

What did we read? We read all the same things other children of that time were reading. But some he merely "tolerated," and to others "gave his gracious consent."

He subscribed to all the then-existing children's magazines—all, from *The Sincere Word*, which he despised, to *The Lighthouse*, which he respected but considered dull. Also *The Guiding Light, The Spring, The Firefly* and *The Path*. They were mainly for himself, in his capacity as a critic, but he didn't hide them from us. As a rule he didn't keep us from reading whatever we wanted, probably thinking us securely defended against banality and mediocrity by Baratynsky, Tyutchev, Pushkin, and Fet.

Generally we read what all boys and girls of our ages were reading at the time. Kolya: Cooper, Mayne Reid, Conan Doyle, Jules Verne, Stevenson, Walter Scott, Dickens, Mark Twain, Hugo. I trailed along after him: only to me Jules Verne, except for *Twenty Thousand Leagues Under the Sea*, seemed unbearably dull, especially *The Children of Captain Grant*. For his part, Kolya was disgusted by my girlish books: *The Little Princess, The*

Blue Heron, Little Lord Fauntleroy, Little Women. I felt that Kornei Ivanovich didn't approve of them either; he teased me about them, but he didn't keep me from reading them. However, I read them to myself, not out loud to him in the evening. It was impossible to read him *The Blue Heron:* he'd make fun of it. Sentimentality, saccharinity, clumsy translations annoyed him. He dreamed of our reading *Alice in Wonderland, Gulliver's Travels, Robinson Crusoe*—but the translations and retellings of these books angered him. For his nighttime reading he chose books which would interest and benefit me without irritating him. Bad translations aroused not drowsiness, but fury.

From my sixth to my tenth year I read him the folktales collected by Afanasiev, then—though these translations also made him frown—the tales of Hauff, Perrault, the brothers Grimm; then the Andersen fairy tales; then *Evenings on a Farm near Dikanka* of Gogol and *Without a Family* of Malot; then we began Mark Twain: *The Prince and the Pauper, Tom Sawyer,* and *Huckleberry Finn;* then novel after novel of Dickens, the novels of Hugo, and a huge amount of poetry, mostly narrative poems, because he was convinced that what children of my age most wanted from poetry and prose was action. He only gave me poetry of the very highest quality: *Red-Nose Frost, General Toptygin, Who is Happy in Russia;* "The Song of the Merchant Kalashnikov," "Borodino," "The Ghost Ship," "The Three Palms;" Russian byliny, *Kalevala* and *Hiawatha.* And *Undine, Nal and Damayanti,* and *The Odyssey* in Zhukovsky's translation.

He considered the ballads of Zhukovsky the basic foundation for the poetic education of the child from eight to twelve and older. Like the folktale, the ballad—in its ancient, original form—was a creation of the people; the world's greatest poets transformed the folk ballad into literature. Every ballad depicts swift action, a whole chain of deeds and events from which it is impossible to tear oneself away. Just exactly what children want, and adolescents, too. He considered ballads as important for adolescents as folktales were for little children. The ballads so beautifully translated into Russian by Zhukovsky sounded natural, so unlike translation, that they were like a second, Russian incarnation of the works of Goethe, Schiller, Walter Scott, Uhland, and Southey: the Russian language he used is sometimes archaic, sometimes colloquial, sometimes literary, but it is always natural and alive. Foreign names for people and places don't add strangeness to the language, just a pleasant touch of mystery: "Brotherstone," "Buccleuch," "quick-running Tweed," "Sir Richard of Coldinghame," "the feast of Poseidon," "Thracian Hills . . ." "Sir Richard of Coldinghame"—the very name sounds like the clang of medieval armor.

Kornei Ivanovich considered the ballads of Zhukovsky—their flexible, resonant, swift-moving, powerfully gripping verses—a superb and necessary school for us. And a holiday as well.

When I turned eleven, in Petrograd, he gave me a three-volume collection of Zhukovsky's work. By that time I already knew by heart "God's Judgment on Bishop Hatton," "The Goblet," and "The Ring of Polycrates." Many were the nights when I was reading to him in Kuokkala that I would light the candle over my favorite favorites: "The Goblet"* or "The Castle of Smaylho'me."**

But I didn't need the candle.

> They crash and they hiss, they whistle and cry,
>> Like water upon fire thrown,
> Wave after wave; then leaps to the sky
>> A streaming column of foam...[9]

Could I possibly forget those lines? And not only I, but also all the Petyas and Ninochkas of my age?

A young man twice throws himself into the boiling foam, but only once can he reach the shore with his precious prize. He will throw himself in a second time and perish. The king's daughter will peer into the boiling waves in vain.

Certainly every girl—one at eight, another at twelve—will, without any cramming, repeat after Schiller/Zhukovsky, with a sad but somehow happy sigh:

> The chasm falls silent...then once more it sounds...
>> And once more it surges with foam...
> A-tremble the princess scans chasm profound...
>> Where breakers so ceaselessly roam...
> Waves come and waves go, in no time whatsoever...
> But not the young man, nor will he come ever.

---

*"The Diver" by Friedrich Schiller. (Translator)
**"The Eve of St. John" by Sir Walter Scott. (Translator)

CHAPTER

XIII

Evening. He hides behind the door of his study. I stand outside the door and await the summons.

Below, in the little entry hall where the stairs begin, hangs a reproduction of Murillo's "Boy with a Dog." The boy's lovely, generous, shy smile follows me upstairs. And above, in the hall next to the study, where I await my call, a poster hangs over the staircase—a red sun with long red rays pasted on green cardboard with yellow letters pasted on it:

> A very springy spring thing
> Amid very springy things.
> A very singy sing thing
> Amid very singy things.

The poet Vassily Kamensky composed, constructed, and hung it here, over our staircase.

"Come in!" says the voice from the study.

Bending over the banister beneath "Spring Thing," I shout down:

> "Papa's going to sleep!
> Let no one make a peep!"

I don't need to shout, except to show off a little; the moment Kornei Ivanovich climbed upstairs, total silence fell downstairs.

When I enter, he is lying in his nightshirt on his huge sofa. Long and narrow, he lies there, his nose buried pitifully in a flat pillow. He looks miserable, his blanket thrown on any old way, his bare feet sticking out. He is filled with a sense of impending insomnia; he is afraid I'll get sleepy and leave before he is able to get to sleep.

"My poor back and feet!" he says to me in a plaintive, capricious voice. This means tuck him in better all the way around. But no sooner do I touch the blanket to cover up his bare feet, than he mischievously, trickily, rolls over on his back and kicks his feet up so high I can't reach them.

His unhappiness has disappeared in a flash; he wants to play before he goes to sleep.

"If you start kicking, you'll never get to sleep," say I didactically. "Lie still."

In answer he lifts his legs even higher and, covering his face with his pillow, begins to snore loudly: see, I'm already asleep.

"If you're going to misbehave," I say. "I'll leave right now. It's past eight."

He obediently lowers his legs, turning on his side again, and I inch around him along the sofa, tucking in the heavy blanket all down his long body.

> —Oh, attention,
> To perfection—
> It is thee!

he singsongs, kicking his just-tucked-in legs one last time.

He's cheered up! That means he's hopeful. If prospects were poor, he'd mutter in a pained, ingratiating voice:

"Oh, how nice . . . oh-oh-oh, what happiness . . . now I'm warm . . . God bless you . . . What a poor boy I am! Christ bless you . . ."

But all this is background, introduction. Time to get down to business.

Ready on the desk are a lighted candle in a square-handled black candlestick, Zhukovsky, opened to "The Castle of Smaylho'me," and next to it, Dickens' *Dombey and Son*. The Dickens—for the real work, for inducing sleep; the Zhukovsky—just because, for getting started, for sheer pleasure.

Matches and a second candle lie at hand just in case. The flame of the burning candle is already well established: tall, even, yellow, and near the wick, dark blue. I set the candle farther away so as not to singe my hair when I bend over the book.

He lies motionless, his cheek on a pillow so thin that from the table where I'm sitting it seems he's lying with his head lower than his body.

Glancing at the book for the sake of appearances, I begin:

> The Baron of Smaylho'me rose with the day,
>> He spurred his courser on,
> Without stop or stay, down the rocky way,
>> That leads to Brotherstone.
>
> He went not with the bold Buccleuch
>> His banner broad to rear;
> He went not 'gainst the English yew
>> To lift the Scottish spear.

> Yet his plate-jack was braced and his helmet was laced,
>   And his vaunt-brace of proof he wore;
> At his saddle-gerthe was a good steel sperthe,
>   Full ten pound weight and more.[1]

I read badly, swallowing words and hurrying to reach my favorite part:

> Come, tell me all that thou hast seen,
>   And look thou tell me true!
> Since I from Smaylho'me tower have been,
>   What did thy lady do?

I couldn't wait for this lady and her secret meetings with the knight, Sir Richard of Coldinghame, near the nighttime beacon light, for the secret murder on the dark highway.

> Yet hear but my word, my noble lord!
>   For I heard her name his name,
> And that lady bright, she called the knight
>   Sir Richard of Coldinghame.

My listener did not think much of my hurried reading. He interrupted me and began to recite the first verse by heart—himself—as a lesson to me. He pronounced each word distinctly and fully, restoring to the lines their stateliness, majesty and even flow. He emphasized the inner rhythm, which I had swallowed:

> ...Without stop or STAY, down the rocky WAY...
> ...yet his plate-jack was BRACED and his helmet was LACED,

he made clear the more hidden sounds:

> To LIFT the Scottish SPEAR...

His recitation brought out both the weight of the armor and the stillness of the horse. The battle axe fixed at the saddle was so heavy it broke the line in two:

> ...a good steel sperthe,
> Full ten pound weight and more.

Following unseen music, he strongly stressed the "EI": "wEIght"—then a tiny pause and then "and more."

101

Full ten pound wEIght
and more.

One other sound stands out in my memory. Everything about "The Castle of Smaylho'me" is mysterious: the nighttime murder, the light of the beacon among the cliffs, the secret meeting with the lover, who "could not come" because he was dead and yet came all the same; the dead hand which, touching the live one, "scorched like a fiery brand;" everything is mysterious, but never mentioned throughout the entire ballad, the mystery is concentrated in one word in one of the last verses:

On her hand . . . but mysteriously from that time on
She did cover her hand with white cloth.

Even now I can hear how Kornei Ivanovich pronounced that word, how he drew it out:

mysTEERiously from that time on

and how he intoned the "EE" as if to help maintain the secrecy in the last, concluding lines:

That was HE, stern murderer, Baron Smaylho'me;
That his young and beautiful wife.

However, I see that he will never get to sleep. He's too wound up. It's high time I got to work. I open up the Dickens, eager, in fact, to find out if Mr. Carker will really manage to marry Florence; or if her good friends, Miss Nipper, Captain Cuttle and Diogenes, the dog, will rescue her. I begin, but he won't let me read, instead he launches into a conversation of some sort about Dickens.

"Now bear in mind," I say firmly. "I'm not about to waste reading on an unsleepy person. Be quiet and listen, or I'll just plain leave."

"Mr. Carker picked his way softly past the house," I read in the flicker of the candle, "and peered intently up at the windows, trying to make out the pensive face behind the curtain, which at that moment was turned toward the rosy children in the house opposite. Diogenes at that moment came clambering up to the window, and catching sight of the passing rider, barked remorselessly, as if he wanted to spring down from the third floor and tear him limb from limb.

"Well done, Diogenes, well done. Defend your mistress. Your head's all dishevelled, your eyes flash, your teeth are bared. Bravo, clever dog!"[2]

"Bravo!" mutters Kornei Ivanovich from his pillow, trying to show that he's not a bit sleepy and is taking an intense interest in Florence's fate.

I keep reading of course, but from time to time I look over at the sofa, and most important, listen to the sound of his breathing. With him one has to keep a sharp lookout, he's capable of all manner of tricks: he can pretend to be sound asleep just to find out if I'm sleepy and ready to abandon him as soon as he begins to breathe regularly.

But so far he hasn't pretended to sleep. Quite the opposite.

"That Diogenes is terrific!" he repeats from his pillow in tones of fake delight: i.e., he's not ready to sleep, he's interested in listening to Dickens.

So I read, and read, and read, now fighting off sleep, now wrapped up in the story, but doggedly keeping track of myself and him: making sure I'm reading slowly, almost monotonously, glancing at his face and listening to his breathing.

"What a poor boy am I!" he says after twenty minutes, throwing the pillow over on its other side and sadly laying his face down on it: "'Poor boy all on fire, all uncomfortable...' What time is it?"

I look at the round black watch, which he usually carries in his pocket, and tell him it's half an hour earlier than it is, so as not to scare him.

Is it possible he won't fall asleep at all tonight?

Meanwhile, Florence and Miss Nipper have unexpectedly shown up at Captain Cuttle's. His landlady happens to be washing the floor of his room at that moment.

"The captain was sitting in the middle of his room as if on a deserted island, washed on all sides by the waters of a soapy ocean...No words can describe the captain's astonishment, when directing his forlorn glance towards the door, he saw Florence and Susan...When Florence came up to the coast of the deserted island and held out a hand to him in a friendly manner, he was dumbfounded and thought at first that a fantastical apparition stood before him."

From the pillow comes the sound of even breathing. Is he asleep? Is he pretending? Just when you're sure, he says something. Last week when I was reading *Bleak House* and he'd seemed sound asleep for fifteen minutes, suddenly his head lifted off the pillow and out of the darkness came:

"If it's the last thing you do—remember: hiLARity, not HIlarity!" and the regular snores began again.

Even in his sleep he kept track of pronunciation!

And how many times has it happened that he's fallen asleep: I stop reading—he doesn't stir; I blow out the candle—he's sleeping; I walk to the door—he's snoring; I leave the room, and for the sake of protocol, stand a minute at the door, beneath "Spring Thing"...And suddenly:

"Ha-ha-ha!" Fake laughter, despairing laughter from behind the door. "She imagined I was asleep. Now, go, go, silly one, it's your bedtime, you're sleepy..."

I would return and beg him to let me to read a little longer, I didn't want to sleep at all—couldn't possibly sleep, any more than if it were morning or afternoon.

He'd let me come back. He was so afraid of being alone! I'd read about an hour longer. He'd fall asleep and sleep all night until morning...What a piece of luck!

But somehow today he can't get to sleep. It seems he's sleeping, then all of a sudden he speaks, laughing at the most inappropriate moment, or to the contrary, exclaiming unhappily and inopportunely (from the pillow): "How sad!" when Dickens is being funny and I can hardly contain my laughter. No, he's not going to fall asleep today!

"'You must certainly be surprised,'" I read, "'to see us here, Captain,' said Florence smiling.

"The delighted captain kissed his iron hook and, not knowing why himself, said, 'Hold tight! Hold tight!' He couldn't come up with a better compliment at that moment."

Quiet, even breathing. I read, and read, and read. Maybe he's fallen asleep? Might as well find out, do an experiment.

I blow out the candle: he's asleep.

Now comes the most difficult part.

In order not to awaken him, I must walk to the door in the dark, and open and close it without interrupting my reading. I must continue to read, read, read.

But how is one to read in the dark?

If I fall silent, he'll immediately wake up, hearing the silence.

I taught myself how to read in the dark. With poetry it wasn't too hard. If I'd just been reading *The Odyssey* for two hours, I could recite in the gloom: "Out of the darkness rose up the young Dawn with her Rose-colored fingers,"—and then any old thing, just so long as it fit the meter: "Here quick Telemachus killed on the spot all the god-loving suitors..."[3]

Prose was more difficult. No meter—that reliable support. And one had to speak without a break. I endeavored to match the original as best I could and, stepping silently across the room, would talk uninterrupted drivel, more afraid of getting tangled in my own nonsense than of running into a chair.

"No words can describe," I say, moving noiselessly in the darkness towards the door, "the picture-framed face of Florence. The reader can easily imagine the evil smile of Mr. Carker, which distorted his lips, which hid his teeth, of which in Captain Cuttle's opinion there were far too many."

I'm at the door. Now if I could just rush downstairs. But no. I must stand there awhile to be sure. The lamp in the entry hall is turned down and I can't see "Spring Thing." But there's a bright light downstairs in the dining room; Boba and Kolya are probably still playing lotto beneath the lamp.

I listen. My heart beats loudly. It's probably been five minutes already. Now if only I can go downstairs successfully, without stepping on the stairs which creak. I know every one, and I always step over them.

The lamp which hangs over the dining room table shines brightly. Boba and Kolya have long ago gone to bed.

"He's asleep!" I say in answer to Mama's questioning look.

That, however, was the happy ending. It often happened that he banished me before he fell asleep. Or sometimes he tricked me; he'd slyly allow me to leave by pretending to be asleep and listen to my nonsense. Then he'd betray me to the boys.

One time, after reading a translation of a French fairy tale as I was making my way to the door in the darkness, I said: "I move away like a beautiful fairy."

He went on snoring. But the next morning! Kolya and Boba met me with a mutual shout of "Beautiful Fairy!" He'd heard every word and told them everything. This nickname hurt more than all the nicknames Kolya dreamed up to taunt me: "Big-long-nosey—Big-round-eyesey," "Mrs. Ticklish," "Liddy the giddy—long-legged biddy."

"Fairy-fay drinks café," said Kornei Ivanovich snidely, alluding to a Chekhov joke.[4]

So, as a young girl, I read to him at night. It was my favorite game. Thus he gave me extra lessons in literature. And maybe I learned something else as well?

Although the words from his Diary were unknown to me at the time: "I ran around my room howling for hours," no one else ever aroused such strong feelings of pity in me, as—from my childhood!—did my healthy, happy, lucky, fortune's-darling of a father.

CHAPTER

XIV

Marshak said of one sorry methodologist, a peevish, tiresome, melancholy fellow, further graced by a pockmarked face and dark blue glasses: "He's pockmarked on principle and shortsighted by conviction."

Kornei Ivanovich was innately cheerful, sociable and drawn to people. Such was his nature. And such he was "by conviction" and "on principle." He set great store by cheerfulness and benevolence, and cultivated them diligently. In himself and others. He loved and valued people who were fun-loving, generous and kind. In his lexicon the word "cheerful" was almost as laudatory as "talented," and boring and boredom were equivalent to mediocre and untalented.

In his article "To Mothers on Magazines for Children," he praised the magazine *The Lighthouse* with the following reservation: "*The Lighthouse* has a secret flaw, which I'll whisper to you—it's boring.

"Certainly, 'arts and crafts' are worthwhile, 'children, don't hurt animals!'—even more estimable, but if only something daring, spirited, reckless might burst upon these pages, to divert children, delight them a little—it would be a lot less oppressive."

And then something daring, spirited, reckless did burst forth, but not on the pages of *The Lighthouse*, but of another magazine, *For Children*.

Until that moment, it was well-known that a crocodile is a dirty-greenish-brown animal, who lives in the rivers and riverbank mud of Africa. Well, maybe also in a zoo, lying just like a log in a special bathtub. But a crocodile that walks upright! And on the streets of Petersburg, on snobbish Nevsky Boulevard! Who smokes cigarettes, speaks German, and casually swallows police constables! Unheard of! It made your head spin!

> Now look who's here
> Suddenly near
> A constable in all his gear:
> For him it was no trial
> Inside the crocodile.[1]

Only a fit of reckless merriment could produce such lines.

There is much to analyze in Kornei Chukovsky's first book for children: the poem's links to Russian and English folklore, its rhythmic and metrical relationship with classical Russian poetry, the whimsy of the story, the victory of good over evil, but the first thing one must say is that with *Crocodile* there burst into the lives of millions of children the irrepressible good cheer of its author.

He couldn't stand boredom in life any more than in books. He didn't like frowning faces, didn't approve of people who dwelt on their misfortunes. In his tales, goodness always wins out, and along with goodness, fun—for him this was not deliberate, but quite natural, particularly since he had sworn fealty to art in his earliest years and believed art was always victorious. (Art was like the lantern which with its light rescued the unfortunate fly from the clutches of the spider.)

"Poor duffer," said he of a critic who made a profession of persecuting in print the works of an excellent poet, "poetry will win out all the same, if not in 1961, then in 1971, if not in '71, then in '81, and he will go down in history as a persecutor of poetry." Kornei Ivanovich made a grimace of disgust. "How distasteful!"

In 1963, in a letter to the poet Peter Semynin, commenting (with great love) on the poems from the book *The Sky's Nearby*, he wrote: "...Like every real poet, you are a prophet, a herald of goodness," and in his conversations he often quoted Whitman:

> Roaming in thought over the Universe, I saw the little that is
>   Good steadily hastening towards immortality,
> And the vast all that is call'd Evil I saw hastening to merge
>   itself and become lost and dead.[2]

"Villains," he said, "are usually idiots. Doing good is always more fun, more interesting, and in the end, more practical."

He was by nature, by birth, sensitive to others and expected sensitivity of himself and those around him. Callousness he considered a deformity. It was not for nothing that he organized during his Peredelkino years a secret society—GDS, "Good Deed Society." President—K.I. Chukovsky, Secretary—F.A. Vigdorova.

From the name Frida, he created the word "Fridism" and "Fridist." We will "save the individual from the savers of humanity," he wrote to one of his correspondents. "Hail Fridism! Join the Fridists!"

He respected the words and the meaning of the words BENignity, BENEvolence, and BENEficence and demanded an amnesty for them.

In an era of revolution, terror and war, Kornei Chukovsky looked around and in a voice slightly slower and quieter than usual said:

Dear good Doctor Help-Me-Please!
Sits right down beneath some trees.
Come and let him look at you
Lady wolf, and cow with flu,
Lowly bug, and little bee,
    And the she-bear, too.
All he treats, and all he sees
Dear, good Doctor Help-Me-Please![3]

Kindness was an integral part of his moral and ethical code, but with a singular twist. To help someone he would tear himself from work, rest, and sleep—without a word of complaint. But there are some diseases which are incurable, some problems which are insoluble. Occasionally it happened that after every remedy had been exhausted, there was nothing left to do but grieve. This he could not do. A good, deserving friend was in trouble—actively, energetically he'd speed to his aid; from the field of a lost battle, from hopeless grief, he'd almost always try to flee. Having done everything possible, even more than was possible, he wanted only one thing—to restore his good spirits and get back to work. He couldn't bear conversation about illness—what this top specialist had said, what that top specialist had said, and what a dangerous bout with appendicitis someone had suffered. "Illness is the least interesting thing about a person," he insisted. "Why do people so love to spend hours talking to each other about where someone hurts?" He didn't like being gloomy and sad and resisted others' attempts to make him feel that way. Sometimes he simply refused to let people talk about injuries, bad luck, and calamities in his presence, protecting with this injunction his work, and with his work, his good spirits. . . . This combination of self-protectiveness and active sensitivity created problems for many people, stumped them. In fact, it sometimes bordered on cowardice, sometimes—strange to say!—even cruelty. I can remember one occasion in the late thirties, after he'd moved to Moscow, when he went up to Leningrad to try to help a man who was in trouble. He was so agitated he didn't sleep the night before he left; as usual he didn't sleep on the train; then was so unhappy when his efforts proved unsuccessful, he didn't sleep in Leningrad. He returned thoroughly exhausted, and after catching a few hours of sleep in his apartment on Gorky Street in Moscow, headed straight for his dacha. The relatives of the man for whom he'd made his difficult trip were waiting for him in Moscow. They had calculated the hours and minutes, had studied the train schedule. He didn't go to them, didn't telephone them, didn't send anyone to them; he went out to his dacha and buried himself in a set of galley proofs. To their utter amazement, they tracked him down there and learned the bitter news.

I remember being astounded by this incident.

"You were undoubtedly very tired," I said. "But couldn't you have sent me to them when you went out to Peredelkino?"

His answer was most unexpected.

"No," said he. "I wasn't tired. I'm just used to bringing people joy . . ."

Magical gift! Lofty ambition! Happy custom! But this time he'd had to bring grief. He didn't want to. His rescue mission had failed, so he went back to work and demanded that no one, at least for awhile, remind him of what had happened.

His intention to bring only pleasure to others and to himself sometimes caused both Kornei Ivanovich and other people a great deal of pain.

His relations with people were far from idyllic.

Usually the blame for this lay with others—and perhaps with the impulsiveness of his generosity. Heaven knows what he imagined in his first, thirsty, curious look at a new person; he would shower that person with excessive warmth; then later tear his hair—the new acquaintance was an ordinary good-for-nothing! Just as obstinate, just as false, just as quick to take offense as most! Extricating himself from a false relationship inevitably meant insulting the other person. But it was a pity to insult someone. He would avoid him, equivocate, confuse others and cause pain.

Here the blame was mutual.

Quite often, all the blame was his; he'd offend people who didn't deserve it at all. Sensitivity—the ability to respond with rare intensity to every appeal—is a precious attribute, but it sometimes turned into inconstancy.

Was it because, despite all his interest in people, he felt profoundly lonely? Was it because he basically didn't believe there was any deeper way of relating to people than through art? And subordinated himself completely to his work? Or finally, was it because the humiliation he'd suffered in his youth permanently distorted his trust in others and in himself? Taught him to be indirect? Whatever the reason, his friendships were characteristically uneven, explosive; the only person who could remain his friend was one who could goodnaturedly withstand ebb tides. The ebbing of what? Not of sympathy, but of intense, focused attention. After all, the passenger who wishes to become acquainted with everyone on the train, no matter how many—not just in the car, but in the whole train—can hardly be expected to spend extended and concentrated time with the people in his compartment.

On occasion, Kornei Ivanovich's sociability and responsiveness hurt his friends deeply, made them feel discarded. Yesterday, and even this morning he had looked at you with such interest and understanding! "And now he hardly seems to see you." You'd like to ask why! But Kornei Ivanovich laughs off the question or dodges it. The person feels unfairly neglected and tries to find a reason for the change, for the ebb tide; the less sensible person—in some sort of secret intrigue or machination, the more intelligent one—in himself. More than likely, the reason lies in the whimsical nature of Kornei Ivanovich. He wrote and said of himself that he worked like a multiple operator, a factory worker who operated *many* machines all at once. And he was the same in his social relations. Plurality. Variety, diversity of interests and attachments, the ability to look at every object, at every thought, at every person, and at every deed from ten, from a hundred points of view all at once constituted his vitality, richness, charm—and also his major shortcoming. It was as if he twinkled and rippled. In the plurality of his perceptions, nuances, feelings, and thoughts, he seemed to have lost or never had the power to see only one aspect of an idea, phenomenon, object or person—specifically, the decisive, most important aspect. He had enormous breadth and independence of intellect, despised bias of any kind, anything which smacked of one-sidedness, one-track-mindedness; he, like no one else, could understand—and accept!—each person and every opinion on each and every thing—and this breadth manifested itself as vacillation, inconstancy, unreliability, indirectness, and it caused his friends severe pain.

Wishing to delight—he injured.

He especially injured those who were lacking in spiritual generosity, those who wished that the branches of this whimsical shade tree might shade only the people close to it, and not, for God's sake, spread its branches across the fence to benefit the chance passerby.

In fact, despite the liberal spreading of its branches, the tree grew straight. Both in literature and in life, Kornei Ivanovich set an example of inconstant constancy. Glancing superficially: what did he not write about! The eye is dazzled: "Shevchenko, Whitman, wind-sailing" says the Chukovsky character in a comic drama by Blok in *Chukokkala*. Looking deeper: he gave whole decades to the study of two or three of his favorite writers, to the repeated working out of selected, favorite themes.

And the same in life. He couldn't pass a new person by. And what a lot there were! But the test of time proved him loyal to the same group of people. He had reason to say proudly and firmly before his death, dictating his will: "No one has had such strong friends as I."

. . .He did not believe in bearing grudges, fought it in himself and others. He remembered every service rendered him, but refused to make anything of a slight—it wasn't productive! He couldn't bear explaining relationships, except perhaps in letters; he avoided directness in conversation. It was as if he wiped the slate clean of slights, his own and others, threw them into oblivion, wiped them from the glass through which he looked out at the world, and he expected others to do the same. How to explain more clearly? He didn't feed on insults, although, of course, he remembered them. Against his will. He did his best to insure that others, too, found different nourishment.

"You're still angry?" he'd say to me, half-sympathetically, half-scornfully, hearing that I didn't wish to see someone who'd injured me. "Is there really nothing you can do? In your place, I'd have forgotten long ago."

If you complained about someone's shocking behavior, protested it, condemned it, he'd wave his long hand and quote Blok: "I see things more kindly and more hopelessly . . ."[4]

Seeing that I was upset, worried: "You should go to the film festival . . . Or 'reread *The Marriage of Figaro.*'"[5]

(Dispose of, dispose of the distress, the worry—get rid of it however you can.)

He is told about some unpleasantness aimed at him. He draws himself up to his full height, and affecting haughtiness, a characteristic he lacked entirely, loftily answers: "I don't have a microscope strong enough to see that louse!"

(Pure theater for himself. He keenly felt such stings, taking to hauteur only as a form of self-protection.)

This was not easy for him, because he was never blessed with the equanimity, evenness of temper, and serenity which are called the temple of wisdom. Just the opposite: despite his bent for fun, he was nervous, excitable, and hot-tempered.

In one of his literary-historical articles, Kornei Ivanovich calls Nekrasov a "genius of depression." Of Kornei Ivanovich it can be said that in his life he was a master of despair. Quite literally, despair—deep, stormy despair, which he would fall into all of a sudden, as one might fall into a hole. For good reason hyperbole was a basic feature of his literary style. Sharp swings from joy to despair often occurred. A person enjoying superb health, spoiled by it, he had become so accustomed to it that he took every cold for pneumonia, every stomach upset for dysentery, every pimple for a malign tumor. And since he did not wish to talk about his illness, would sit down manfully to write his will. Starting in his fifties, every time a page of writing gave him trouble, he'd announce that it was all over, that sclerosis had set in and he couldn't write another line, that his literary life was over. (At age eighty-five sclerosis still hadn't caught up with him!) In a heartrending voice, he would announce the immediate end of his life and literary career. Though when the cold he was coming down with of an evening, next morning proved nothing more than a cold, he'd show a guest from porch to gate in twenty-below weather wearing his coat open and without a hat ("The host himself in stately fashion went out onto the porch"), and if you insisted he put on his hat, he'd throw it in the snow, shouting he had no need for a guardian; and when a page which had stumped him for a long time finally worked out, expressed so smoothly it appeared written in one stroke of the pen, then he'd be convinced that sclerosis hadn't yet deprived him of his literary skills, and he'd be able to write several portraits for his *Contemporaries*, rewrite *Alive as Life*, add to *From Two to Five* for the hundredth time and to *The High Art* for the tenth, finish his lifelong work on Chekhov and redo his translations of Whitman—oh, what wild exultation he could indulge in, instantly forgetting yesterday's brink-of-death despair.

Having escaped disaster, *The Boldly Buzzing Fly* would celebrate his name day once again.

Peredelkino. Ten o'clock in the morning. He got up at five. He's working. Now it's breakfast time. We await him downstairs in the dining room.

The Peredelkino staircase rises to the second floor in just the same way the Kuokkala staircase did.

—Having skimmed off his fee most unethical,
My attorney became hypothetical,

was heard from the stairway.

There stands in your presence a being,
Pure as snow from the Alps all serene![6]

He's in a good mood! That means he was able to sleep and to work. And the pimple—it was only a pimple.

If he doesn't come down to breakfast for a long time, you go up and knock on his door:

"Breakfast time, Gramps!"

"Just turning off the lamps!" he replies.

Everything's okay. Wonderful! He slept and worked.

Coming down the stairs, he recites in songlike fashion:

—Three hundred years soon Gramps will be,
Oh, what a pistol still is he!

Another day you call to him: "Grand-pa!"

"Yes, Grandma?" he answers vindictively. You enter. He's in black despair. Sclerosis—time to throw away the pen—he's no longer a writer. He doesn't want to come downstairs, and doesn't want anyone to bring his breakfast upstairs. He has stomach cancer or dysentery. Despair.

A master of despair... Genuine, enormous. In Moscow, with my own eyes, I saw him spend an entire day, from dawn to dusk, lying on the floor after receiving an insulting letter from some literary person; he wouldn't stand up, wouldn't move to the sofa, wouldn't go out for a walk—he assured us that the man who had offended him was right, he was a nothing, pitifully lacking in talent, and as a result he was going to spend the rest of his life lying on the floor... The incident ended with his getting up at night when nobody could see him and sitting down at his desk to work. He worked until morning, without a break. (He hurried to make up for lost time. Punished himself for giving in to despair.)

He took his most reliable medicine: completed several pages.

If someone said in his presence that "they weren't in a mood to work that day," he would curl his lip disdainfully. He would admit to no "moods." He considered it merely a petty excuse, unworthy of a professional writer.

"If you worked ten hours straight, then you'd be in a good mood."

Work was his cure not just for attacks of literary despair, but also for the most incurable of sorrows.

...In 1920, in a cold and hungry Petrograd winter, his second daughter was born, his fourth child. He became tremendously attached to Murochka: both because she was frail, barely surviving her infancy, and also because she had inherited unmistakable literary talent. At the age of eleven, in the Crimea, after long suffering, Murochka died of tuberculosis in his and her mother's arms. At the time of her death, despairing, sobbing letters arrived from the Crimea. I can remember by heart the beginning of one of them, which unfortunately has been lost:

"When I look at Murochka, I envy parents whose children fall from the sixth floor or are run over by a tramcar in the street..."

Murochka's tuberculosis first affected her legs, then an eye; then it spread to her kidneys, then her lungs, and only after all that did it kill her.

Kornei Ivanovich did everything he could to save her, to care for his sick child, but did not for one day stop working: he wrote a short story about the sanatorium where Murochka stayed for several months. He gave the story a cheerful name: "Sunny."

Similarly in 1942, in evacuation in Tashkent, when he learned of Boba's death, he never stopped working: he gave lectures, he wrote about children in evacuation.

The same was true in 1965 when his oldest son, Nikolai Korneyevich, died suddenly in his sleep. He lay down after dinner, fell asleep and never woke again. Three days earlier he had been perfectly healthy, had gone to visit his father in a sanatorium. Then he was gone, and relatives brought the dreadful news to his father.

The sorrowful entry in his diary ends this way: "...Oblonskaya came, we edited Walt Whitman and that was my salvation. All day we worked on *Leaves of Grass*—she is bright, hard-working, and I am keeping a tight grip on myself."

Work kept grief at bay, shielded him, helped him "keep a tight grip on himself." And further, it raised his resistance by requiring him to lift his spirits.

"I have no doubt that every article you write comes only with bloody torment, but at the same [time] experiencing this torment is a *pleasure*. The torment and the pleasure are felt in every line you write."

Kornei Ivanovich wrote these words to the young critic Valentin Nepomnyashchy, whose articles he much admired.

These words describe himself.

I never saw a writer for whom writing was more difficult: in his youth, as much as in his later years. Achieving simplicity, clarity, smoothness and force in the expression of subtle and complex thought caused him "bloody torment," insomnia, hard work. Hard but happy.

"I am overcome here by a level of 'happiness in work,'" he wrote in his diary in 1909 upon arriving at a dacha with a separate tower, "which I have not experienced in three years. I am redoing Garshin completely—the article about him—and joyfully look forward to setting to work again tomorrow. I'm going to bed now, and will read myself to sleep with *The Idiot*...Is there anyone who is happier than I..."

Not just joy, but a degree higher—true happiness. That was in 1909. And sixty years later, in 1969, in the spring of his last year, one day I went out on the balcony, where he'd been sitting, writing, since early morning wrapped in a plaid blanket—I went out to call him to breakfast.

"Look," I couldn't help saying, "what a wonderful day it is today, the sky, the leaves just beginning to appear!"

Tossing off the blanket, he stood up and looked at the sky, at the birchtree where a mother squirrel and her young were occupying a starling house instead of starlings, and said firmly, solemnly, and joyfully, without the slightest touch of irony: "We must show our gratitude for this day with work!"

And straightening up, he rubbed his back as though he'd just been sawing wood.

But his eternal striving for cheerfulness of spirit and the happiness of work did not keep him aloof from people's troubles. (As long as something could be done about them.) How it was possible to combine these two aims, I don't know. But whether happy or sad, he was keenly aware of other people's problems, never blind to them. (Although to all the world's troubles and joys, he preferred one happiness, one narcotic—work.)

Peredelkino. Again we are walking along a road together as we did in Kuokkala—not along the level Big Road in Kuokkala, but the ascending Peredelkino roadway. It is a day of mourning, the anniversary of the death of my mother, who died in 1955. That was probably the heaviest loss of his life. February. As usual on this day, a blizzard. The wind blows. "The blizzard blinds our eyes."[7] In the deep snow, making our way among fenced-in plots, we climb up to a fence which surrounds one grave with space for another beside it.

Kornei Ivanovich stands on the spot where he will be lowered into the ground.

I can't help looking at him, alive and healthy though he is, as if at his future ghost.

Sometimes he stands there without speaking, sometimes begins to crack jokes. About his own funeral. About his own future neighbors. Sometimes he explains exactly how I must handle his burial. And stamps with his felt boots: here.

(Death did not frighten him: several years later, when it came to his bedside and he understood that he was dying, he met it with dignity. Much more calmly than he usually faced a cold.)

I want to leave the graveyard as quickly as possible, to escape my double image: here he stands, safely alive in the snow, I see him and hear him, yet at the same time I see a hole beneath his feet, hear other voices, see a coffin being lowered.

I long to go back down the hill with him. He has caught cold so often in recent years! Snow has collected in his felt boots and on his shoulders, his collar is wet. Today he is filled with bitter memories, gloomy presentiments. He stands fixedly, staring at the white mound.

At last I'm able to lead him away. We go down the hill, with one hand I hold his hand, which is as warm as ever, with the other, take hold of frozen fenceposts. He walks in silence, downcast, old, his face a grayish color, his lips blue...I want to get home as fast as possible, where it will be warm, and he'll be able to take off his boots, put on warm socks, drink tea with raspberry preserve, and take some valocardin for his heart.

We have reached the bottom of the hill. Here's the bridge over the Setun. Fifteen minutes more and we'll be home.

We walk on one side of the bridge, a man shuffles along on the other. He is young, but all bent over. He moves heavily, drags his feet, his head lowered toward the bridge.

Suddenly, without straightening or turning his head to us, speaking with his face to the bridge: "If only you could help me, Kornei Ivanovich."

To me Kornei Ivanovich seems in imminent need of an ambulance. He's very weak. But I'm wrong. Quickly and lightly he crosses the bridge. He's tall, strong, energetic, just as he'd been in the storm on the Gulf of Finland.

"What's wrong with you? What happened?"

We're on the road now, walking together, the three of us. Kornei Ivanovich shortens his step to match the slow, heavy tread of the young man.

Turns out he's a plumber. His back is in great pain, but "the doctors can't find anything wrong," "pitch vitamins at him." They have promised to put him in the hospital for tests, but there's no room, never any room.

Kornei Ivanovich climbs up the steps to the workers' dormitory with him. He takes down his first name, last name and address...Then as soon as we return home, without changing his shoes or eating lunch, he begins telephoning the nearest hospital, in Solntseva, with the help of Klara Israelevna.

No bed is available, but they promise one as soon as possible. After several days, a call from the hospital: they have a bed but no transportation.

Kornei Ivanovich offers his own car.

A few days later comes the news: the man is suffering not from lumbago, as they had thought at the polyclinic, but from cancer. Cancer of the spine. There is no way to save him. All they can do is lessen his pain. And although they have painkillers at the hospital, they have none strong enough to do the job.

Another set of letters, sent into town right away with the chauffeur, a new set of telephone calls. The strongest painkillers are found.

Such behavior was routine for him.

(One qualification is necessary at this point—regarding the telephone. Kornei Ivanovich was a passionate telephone-hater. Throughout his life he had acute telephonophobia. It was impossible to imagine him conversing with someone by phone in the same comfortable way he loved to talk with people face-to-face. He was so adamantly against this form of communication, he often confounded the people who phoned him: he'd pick up the receiver, say a few words, then without finishing his thought or listening to the answer, hang up without a goodbye or any concluding phrase; the person on the other end would be left as up in the air as if the connection had been broken. He tried different approaches in his battle against the telephone. In Leningrad one day when I went into his study for a book, I heard a gurgling sound coming from his desk. He was sitting there writing, and in the drawer something was gurgling. I listened: it was definitely a human voice. Seems Kornei Ivanovich had picked up the receiver and said hello, but his work was progressing apace, and he couldn't talk: he closed the receiver in a desk drawer so he wouldn't hear the voice and continued to write. Once in a while he would pull the receiver out of the draw and say persuasively: "Marvelous! I agree with you completely," then hide that other voice away again in the drawer, fussing at the cord which would not allow him to close the drawer all the way.

Soon we moved the telephone to a different room—a long way from him!—and began to answer it ourselves, trying to shield him from calls. But, a lady phones a seventh time without identifying herself and insists on speaking to Kornei Ivanovich. I call him. I'm tired of lying and saying he's not at home.

"You really couldn't come up with any way to rescue me?" he answers, irritated. Then suddenly an inspiration, like a miraculous invention, like a line for a poem, in a splendidly clear voice audible in every corner of the large Leningrad apartment: "Te-ell her that I'm already de-ead and bur-ied in the Vo-olkov Cemetery!")

Peredelkino forced him to come to terms, at least to an extent, with the telephone. All his business, all the publishing houses, everything of the sort was in Moscow. It was impossible to get along without the telephone. Especially in his last years when he stopped going into Moscow entirely. Certainly, Klara Israelevna and the rest of us, looking after him in turn, would screen his calls and try not to burden him with the telephone. But all the same, business, his own and others', often forced Kornei Ivanovich to use that much-despised instrument. He would wait while Klara Israelevna or Marina Nikolaevna got through all the required names and numbers, while they connected him with the city, then would take the receiver.

"This is Chukovsky, the writer. . .Is this the Second Surgical Ward? The head nurse? Please be good enough to call the head of the department to the telephone. Nina Mikhailovna? Yes, Chukovsky. . .You saw Marshak? I'm so happy for you. Perhaps it wouldn't be a bad idea to catch a glimpse of Chukovsky, too. . .Don't miss your chance. . ." (He listens impatiently, but he mustn't hang up.) "Your Mishenka knows *Scrub-n-Rub* by heart? A-ma-zing! You've got a real genius for a child. . .Bring him to see me in Pere-delkino. Just drop in. . .I'll sign a copy of *The Boldly Buzzing Fly* for Mishenka and a copy of my book on Chekhov for Mishenka's mother. . . Yes, imagine that, I write on other things beside little tiny cockroaches. . . Nina Mikhailovna, would you be so kind, may God watch over you forever, an old friend of mine, Lyubov Grigoryevna Baranovskaya, is lying there in your corridor. She was a doctor who devoted her whole life to medicine. Now she's over eighty. An accident, in the street, a broken pelvis. Be so good as to look after her personally, arrange a consultation, and most important, dear friend, from your voice I can tell you're a warmhearted, sympathetic person—if it's at all possible, move her out of the corridor into a room. . .Deepest regards to Mishenka!"

And he would put his hand to his heart with sincerity. And exhausted, hang up the phone.

Or it might go like this: "Ivan Petrovich? It's the writer Chukovsky speaking. There's been some kind of misunderstanding about a student who has applied to your department, Grisha Beskin. . .Not CHULkovsky—CHUKovsky. Yes, yes, the very one." (Pause. Kornei Ivanovich listens impatiently. The man on the other end, as can be deduced from the rest of the conversation, is telling him that his wife also writes poems for children.) "What a happy coincidence! You both ought to come see me in Peredelkino, we could recite together. . .Any Sunday. Zinochka knows all of *The Boldly Buzzing Fly* by heart? Remarkable! I'd love to meet such an ex-tra-or-din-a-ry child! I'll give her a copy of *Cock-the-roach*, and your wife a copy of my Whitman translations. Yes, imagine that, I do write about something other than hippopotamuses. Ivan Petrovich, I've known Grisha Beskin since he was a baby. He's a natural-born historian. He was over at my house not long ago and spoke about the Scythians wonderfully well. He's a well-read boy with an inquiring mind. Just made for the study of history. . .And he didn't pass his entrance exam in history. His mother's in tears. There must have been some kind of misunderstanding. As a special favor to me, Ivan Petrovich, could you look into the situation yourself, I've heard so much about your perspicacity and goodness. . ."

Thus he would involve himself in other people's lives, trying to bring them joy. His letters and phone calls on behalf of others to publishing houses, to the Moscow City Council, to the Public Prosecutor's Office, or to the Writer's Union would fill many volumes. Bringing joy to others was his way of insuring his own joy. The feeling was as necessary to him as oxygen. Cheerfulness. This need could pull him out of the deepest gloom.

...Again the day of mourning: February. Again, as always, a blizzard on this day. Again we're on the road, then at the grave—the two graves, the real one and the future one. He's in despair. Hasn't written this, hasn't rewritten that. As we are walking the path down the hill, he begins that most unbearable of all conversations—about his burial. What I must do when he dies.

"Yes, yes," I mutter quickly. "I'll certainly...Don't worry, we'll do.... Come on, let's talk about this at home. I won't forget. Don't worry. I give you my word."

I realize I must change the subject right away. After all it's easy to distract him! When we reach the bridge, I snatch the first idea that pops into my head.

"Remember," I say thoughtlessly, "exactly a year ago, on this same day, on this same bridge, we met the man..."

"Yes," he answers dryly. "The man asked for my help, and I didn't help him. He died."

"But you got medicine for him to relieve his pain. There is no medicine to cure cancer!"

None—so why did I have to bring it up?

Kornei Ivanovich walks beside me on unsteady old legs, contending against the wind with difficulty. Gloomy, frail! I wasn't able to distract him from his bleak thoughts. Just the reverse. I have plunged him deeper into gloom.

But not for long. When we get back to the house, the entry hall is full of scarves and hats. Children fill the dining room. Seventh graders from a Moscow school have come for a visit with their teacher. Twenty-five of them. They look at him curiously, shyly, expectantly.

"What bad timing," I think to myself, "he ought to go lie down."

But he doesn't see the children's invasion that way at all. For him it is a healing source of joy.

In a trice another of his natural talents comes to life—acting.

Playfully, he tosses his coat and hat on the pile of scarves, hats and coats, and under the eager eyes of his audience, seats himself on the sofa in the dining room.

"Kla-arka!" he cries in a loud voice, clapping his hands three times.

The typewriter upstairs falls silent. The children watch him intently.

"Who knows when serfdom was abolished? In 1861! Right! A hundred years ago! But here at my house it still continues. I'll show you! 'Hey, Ivan!' Klarka, come here! Take off the old man's boots!"

Klara Israelevna, who never knew from minute to minute what he might cook up next but was always ready to take part in anything, with a smile knelt before him on the rug and helped take off his boots. He pretended that it hurt, grimaced horribly, and shoved her shoulder lightly with his boot.

She laughed. The children too.

The game had begun.

"Hey, Ivan, my slippers!" cried Kornei Ivanovich.

In a minute Klara Israelevna had brought his slippers down from upstairs.

"Oh-ho!" he threatens, waving his forefinger at her, as he had once waved it at me. Then he stamps his feet on the rug.

> "'It's my fault!' a trifle meekly
> Mumbled out Ivan.
> 'Fix some goose for dinner quickly,
> And some soup, you dolt, anon!'[8]

Are you convinced? Call them all upstairs!"

He takes the children upstairs to his study to read them some Nekrasov and maybe, if he finds them responsive, Blok.

He stands for a long time, rubbing his lips with the backs of long hands, as if he's getting ready to kiss someone; then he pretends to give the teacher a big kiss, and standing back, exclaims: "He placed a kiss on her rosy lips!" or putting an arm around her shoulder: "Darling, at last we're alone!" or "We'll not tell a soul about us!"[9] or:

> From the old man she lures lavish presents,
> The young man's hopelessly smitten with love.[10]

He must show the children the engine which knows how to go around chairs, and the lion which can speak, and Humpty-Dumpty sitting with his legs hanging down, not on a wall, but on some books, on a shelf over the ottoman. He seeks out and observes the most lively and intelligent of the children and asks the teacher about them—learning from her answers about her as well as about them.

Once again on this day of mourning, he recovers his own joy by giving joy to others.

CHAPTER
XV

I know of only one pain which, though he never talked about it, Kornei Ivanovich never forgot, never put aside, one injury which he allowed himself to nurse.

Cheerfulness, the desire to consign troubles and slights to oblivion, were hopeless in this case. And so were the satisfactions of work.

This indelible pain was his resentment against his father for the unpardonable fate of his mother and sister, for his own stolen childhood.

"I was born in Petersburg in 1882, and soon afterwards, my father, a Petersburg University student, abandoned my mother, a peasant woman from the Poltava Province; and she moved with her two children to Odessa." Thus writes Kornei Chukovsky in a short autobiographical essay at the beginning of his *Collected Works*.

My grandfather, my father's father, was never mentioned in our house, not under any circumstances, not at any time, not for any reason. Throughout his long life, Kornei Ivanovich never spoke of him at all in conversation, and only twice mentioned him in print: in the just-quoted essay, "About Myself," and in his story "The Silver Crest." In both cases it was mentioned in order to write "he abandoned" and then to describe the fate of those who were abandoned.

I am not writing Kornei Ivanovich's biography. I am writing about my childhood, and he was its creator. He and my childhood—no matter how old he was or I was—were inseparable. Looking at his hands in his coffin, I saw them on the oars in Kuokkala. And he, the sort of person he was and the kind of childhood he created for us, was created by his abandonment. That's why I cannot not write about it. It was a fundamental aspect of the way he related to children, his own and others', the source of his insatiable desire to enrich children, to endow them so that they would never, under any circumstances, become "poor, poor." His childhood abandonment was the direct cause of his lifelong interest in children's lives, his insistence that adults respect and care for children; it gave rise to his books for children, and his book about children for adults, *From Two to Five*. It was the reason for the little library full of toys and books which he built in Peredelkino for the children of the neighborhood. It inspired his constant efforts to insure that we grew up surrounded by culture, not cut off from it. English, poetry, skiing, books.

Everything he had been deprived of as a child, he bestowed upon his children when he became a father.

The wound he suffered in his youth never healed, never ceased to ache.

An entry in his diary attests to the severity of the wound. It was written in 1925, when he was almost forty-three and had already officially changed his name from Nikolai Vasileyvich Korneichukov to Kornei Ivanovich Chukovsky.

During a period of forced and unexpected leisure due to illness, he decided to go through old documents, and rereading them brought back hateful memories of his boyhood and adolescence.

He had not just been robbed, he had been spat upon.

Only one person, and that a fictional one, could possibly have authored this page—the hero of Dostoevsky's novel *The Raw Youth*.

Here's what he wrote:

It's particularly painful to read the Odessa letters written just before I went to London. I tore up all those letters—I would happily have obliterated that time as well. My total lack of direction was frightening, my lack of belonging—I did not even have a name . . .As an illegitimate child, I. . .was the most divided, most complicated person in the world. The main reason was that during those years I was too excruciatingly ashamed to say that I was illegitimate. . .First of all, admitting I was illegitimate meant disgracing my mother. I felt that. . .I was the only illegitimate child in the world, that everyone else was legitimate, that everyone was whispering behind my back, and that when I showed my papers to anyone (a caretaker, a porter) he would immediately begin to despise me. And, in fact, that was the case. I remember. . .the agonies of that time:

"What is your station?"

"I'm a peasant."

"Your papers?"

Terrible words appeared in those papers: son of a peasant, *Miss* so and so. I was so afraid of those papers, I never read them myself. It was terrible even to look at those words. I remember how insulting, how shameful I found the school-leaving certificate given my sister Marusya, the best student at our diocesan secondary school; on the certificate was written: "a peasant's daughter, Maria (*no patronymic*) Korneichukova—with highest honors." I can still remember how that...pierced me with shame. "We are not like other people, we are worse, we are the lowest of the low,"—and when children talked about their fathers, grandfathers, grandmothers, I just blushed, mumbled, lied, got tangled up. I'd never had the luxury of a father, or even a grandfather. The lie, the muddle, I lived at that time was the source of all my lies and falsehoods later on in life. Now when I come upon any of my letters to anyone, I can see the letters were illegitimate...The worst time of all was when I was sixteen and seventeen...I remember the clownlike way I said to everyone, even on first acquaintance—though I already had a mustache, "Just call me Kolya," "And I'm Kolya," etc. It seemed buffoonery, but it was misery.

It was misery and it remained so—in the grown man, the middle-aged man, and the old man—despite the consolation of the new name, which he created for himself, chose for himself, and made official after the revolution.

In the Kuokkala time, when according to his papers he was still the son of "Miss Ekaterina Osipovna Korneichukova," the misery continued unrelieved; his love and pity for his mother, and the deep respect he felt for her, rooted in his childhood, made him look on his father as an enemy.

He could not fight this feeling of enmity.

I remember in Kuokkala, when I was about six and Kolya nine, our mother, Maria Borisovna, took us into her bedroom unexpectedly one day, shut the door tightly, and said for no apparent reason: "Now I want you to remember this, children. You must never ask your father anything about his father, your grandfather. Nothing at all. Do you hear? Now don't forget."

To be honest, we hadn't been planning to ask: until that moment it hadn't occurred to us that we didn't have the full complement of relatives. We knew that Mama's papa, one of our grandfathers, had died about the time Boba was born, but neither Kolya nor I had ever seen him. Mama's mama, our grandmother, was alive, but we'd seen only her photograph and letters. Once in awhile our Aunt Marusya, Papa's sister, and Aunt Zinochka, Mama's sister, would come to Kuokkala. Mama also had another sister, Aunt Natasha. Of all our close relatives the only one we knew well and loved was Papa's mother, Ekaterina Osipovna. She came every year and stayed for a long time; she was a handsome, dignified, stately woman with capable hands; she prepared tasty pies, made cookies and poppyseed buns with honey, and baked the most wonderful kulich! (Grandmother even sent kulich to London, so we'd been told, when Papa married and went there with Mama to be correspondent for an Odessa paper.) If Grandmother came at Easter time, then blue, green, red and yellow "painted" eggs, stacked in a cheerful heap on a platter, would appear on the table, immediately turning our everyday table into a holiday one.

Grandmother Ekaterina Osipovna was religious. We didn't worship icons in our house and didn't go to church, but so as not to offend grandmother, the day before her arrival her favorite icon, Nicholas the Miracle Worker, would be hung in the children's room, where she slept along with Boba and me, and a candle would be lit.

We would run happily to greet her at the train station. She didn't bring us toys, but she did bring lots of cherry jam without pits. Kornei Ivanovich would with difficulty lift her heavy woven basket off the train, then motion to the cabman.

Papa and Grandmother resembled each other. Both had wide black eyebrows and bright green eyes, but Grandmother was shorter and a good deal better looking.

When Papa emerged from his study with his hair mussed, she'd say to him: "Brush the hair off your forehead!" and with an imperious hand smooth back his forelock.

He, so much taller than she, would lower his head submissively, as if he were little all over again.

Deaf to Mama and Papa's loud objections, Grandmother would set to work the moment she arrived: making me aprons, darning Papa's socks and our stockings. She couldn't sit idle for a moment. She'd starch the curtains and the tablecloth in her own special way.

...I don't know about Kolya, but at six, I wasn't too sure how many grandmothers and grandfathers a person was supposed to have. After Mama talked to us, I wondered for the first time about our grandfather, Papa's father. And why we mustn't ask about him.

"That grandfather probably died," I said to Kolya after Mama's injunction.

"Nonsense. Double nonsense. Mama's papa died, and she talks about him. His picture's on the bureau. Aunt Zina talks about him, too. For some reason we can't talk about this one."

"Maybe he was in prison?" I asked. "He's hiding. He's afraid. When someone's been to prison, you're not allowed to talk about them either."

But an order's an order. Like the other relatives we'd never seen, Grandfather didn't interest us particularly, and we easily obeyed Mama's command.

However, two years passed, and then all of a sudden and similarly unexpectedly Mama announced: "Kolya will move out of the schoolroom and sleep downstairs, we must prepare the schoolroom for a guest. Papa's father is coming to visit us tomorrow for two weeks."

"Will we be able to talk to him?" I asked.

The next day our neighbor Kollyari's carriage drove up to the gate as ordered by Kornei Ivanovich the evening before, and he set out for the station to meet Grandfather.

He went alone. Did not take us with him.

Mama and Nanny Tonya bustled about the kitchen. We committed all the cardinal sins at once: did nothing, made excuses for it, and generally frittered away our time.

We waited.

And then, finally, at the gate—Kollyari, Papa, and Grandfather. Papa carried Grandfather's suitcase. I didn't get a good look at Grandfather; I saw only that he had a beard. I fixed on his hands, full of flowers and packages. Grandfather had brought presents for everyone: for Mama—flowers, for Kolya—a fancy book, for me—a doll, for Boba—a drum.

The table was set. From the kitchen came the smell of pies. But we didn't sit down at the table: Papa took Grandfather upstairs to his study. I went out to the raspberry bush, behind the icehouse to think: what would I do with that doll, how would I dress her, what would I call her? I couldn't bear my dolls (they were all presents from Mama and Papa's acquaintances!), I didn't know how to play with them—I had grown up with boys.

(Before our move to Petrograd I didn't have a single girl friend. Kornei Ivanovich told me that until I was three I talked about myself like Kolya, in the masculine: himself, he ate. With my dolls, I'd usually conscientiously sit them up in the morning in chairs, telling them that, "Mama was going into the city on business," and then not touch them again for the rest of the day.

But I came up with a name for this one quite quickly. I'd call her Florence, Flo.)

Then suddenly the door onto the veranda opened noisily. Kornei Ivanovich burst through it with Grandfather's suitcase in his hands and ran to the gate. Behind him, struggling to keep up, came Grandfather (this time I noticed that he was tall, thinnish, erect and wore a square beard). Kornei Ivanovich went through the gate and opened it wide for his guest. He gave him his suitcase and turned away, closing the gate behind him.

"Why isn't anyone eating lunch?" he shouted at us as he entered the house.

Not a word was said about Grandfather during lunch. Nor after lunch. Nor for the rest of his life. As I learned later, the conversation upstairs in the study had been about Ekaterina Osipovna. About the children, Marusya and Kolya, "who had never had the luxury of a father," about the boy who had been haunted by the knowledge that he, his mother and his sister "were not like other people," were worse than everyone else, "the lowest of the low."

When I turned seventeen, my parents let me visit my grandmother in Odessa. It was the first time I had traveled alone on an overnight train. I arrive at my grandmother's apartment—tiny, sparkling clean. Full of flowers—on the windowsill, on the floor—and on the walls, photographs of Kornei Ivanovich. (At our house most of the pictures of him were caricatures, and only one portrait always hung on the wall, a photograph of the Repin portrait, done in 1910.) Grandmother clearly did not like caricatures, but photographs of her son, even the most fuzzy newspaper one, she would cut out and hang on the wall. Here's the plush-covered family album: pictures of little Marusya and Kolya with Grandmother—oh, how pretty she'd been!—Kolya all by himself, as a gymnasium student, in his student cap still bearing its insignia, everything just as it should be—his overcoat, his knapsack. That means it was taken before he was expelled.

"I already knew my Kolya was a bright boy," sighed Grandmother, "but I couldn't explain it to them."

She had sat six hours in the school director's waiting room. He had seen her—but what can one say to someone carrying out orders from the authorities?

I lift my eyes from the album. There, hanging above a bowl of fig blossoms, is a much-enlarged photograph in a heavy frame. I recognize that same thinnish, attractive man with a carefully trimmed beard. The one we could never talk about.

"Your Papa doesn't like him," said Grandmother, noticing my glance, "because of me. But your Papa's wrong: he's a very, very good man."

Was he a good man? Grandmother loved him all her life and never married anyone else, although she had offers. Was he a bad man? I don't know and it's not for me to judge.

I hope Ekaterina Osipovna was right. But for Kornei Ivanovich his childhood abandonment was the only personal injury he could not prevail against, either with work or with fun.

That is undoubtedly why he cared so much about children all his life.

CHAPTER

XVI

Did Kornei Ivanovich really love children?

What an unnecessary question. Especially after everything that's been recounted here.

What a silly question. It's obvious he loved children. Who doesn't love adorable little ones?

"Children are life's flowers," "Children are our future." And Chukovsky after all! *The Boldly Buzzing Fly, Scrub-n-rub, From Two to Five.* The strong young father with strong arms tossing his son to the ceiling...And then, Dear Grandfather Kornei.

However, though he really did love children, contributed much to them and brightened their lives, the answer is not as simple as it seems at first: he loved them in very much his own way; at any rate, he couldn't stand adults who went into raptures over children—the mamas, papas, uncles who showily caressed their little ones, ostentatiously exchanged kisses with them, gave them tender nicknames, nibbled on them from head to toe with loud kissing and smacking sounds, and showered them with gifts, convinced that they were more intelligent, talented and charming than anyone else's; he couldn't stand ringlets, lace, and white stockings; he wouldn't put up with birthdays, the obligatory presents, cakes, relatives; I don't remember ever seeing him kiss a child, I don't remember his ever caressing me or anyone else when I was a child, though he would place a hand on head or shoulder, playfully threaten with a long forefinger, or take part in the game of "sawing-in-half;" generous as he was about sharing himself with children, his own and others' (after Murochka's death he began regularly to visit sanatoriums and hospitals for children with tuberculosis as well as schools and kindergartens—there was no happier gift for children than his appearance; it was as good as a fully decorated New Year's tree delivered to their bedside!), I don't remember that he, our once-upon-a-time favorite toy, ever gave anyone the gifts most people give children as a sign of affection—a box of chocolates, a doll or a set of soldiers. What he gave as gifts were notebooks, pads, penknives or, like a laurel wreath, a pencil with red and blue leads—in other words, any of the writing utensils which he loved—and sometimes, a quickly sketched funny picture. (He did bring us back from London in 1916 two artistically made dolls: a Scotsman in native costume and a "golliwog.") In general, he believed that having too many toys was bad for children, that it was better not to give presents too often so toys didn't cease being special; he felt that for the most part adults gave children toys to show off, and because it was easy. Just go out, buy, give. It took no real thought for the child. Only money.

Did he really love children?

The child in him never died.

Reading an English book which asserted that sometimes childlike qualities live on in the grown man, he wrote in the margin: "that's me."

He certainly did enjoy hopping to the gate or building castles in the sand. His passion for investigation never wore out. He not only loved children, he was curious about them—the spirit of the scientist, the experimenter, the teacher. Contact with children was always a basic need of his, like food, water, and books. With his own? Yes, with his own, too. But his own weren't enough, he knew them by heart, and he was always drawn to novelty: he was constantly in need of new specimens of childhood to observe, to listen to, and to play with. He said of himself that he "went to children" the way others "went to the people."* He was interested in individual children, of course, but he liked to mix with a multitude even more—with flocks, bands, teams, companies, wards at a hospital, classes at a school. He would watch and listen to children at their lessons, on the road, at work, at play, and most important, team up with them. They were skipping stones—who could skip farthest? He'd try, too. They were climbing trees—who could climb highest? And he! We'd be walking the top of the railroad track—who could go farthest without sliding down the embankment?—he'd join us. He was shoveling snow—okay, Lida, Kolya, Pavka, you shovel, too!

In Kuokkala he had three of his own, and five others, Russians and Finns. Five? No, tomorrow there'll be even more.

In Peredelkino there were children from three different villages, plus whole busloads from Moscow, and still others, jumping from every fence, running from every gate during his slow rambles along the road. With his long arms he'd hug them to himself, three at a time, or if they were small, five, and they'd press their noses into his fur coat. The children of watchmen, chauffeurs, writers, furnace stokers.

"Hello there, Nikita! How about it, did you pass arithmetic?"

"Ninochka! Show me what book you chose today. Why don't you try Andersen next time?"

---

*A reference to Populism, the "Going to the People" movement of the late nineteenth century in Russia. (Translator)

People have studied and written about his importance to children. I want to understand what they were to him, what role they played in his life. His own words provide an answer.

Here are a few citations from his letters and Diary.

Since I met these children. . .all adults have somehow clouded over for me. It's strange, but I can only really relax amongst children.

I have a special way of curing myself of depression and worry: I invite children to come see me and spend five, six, seven hours with them.

Al(exei) Iv(anovich) Panteleev was visiting me, and we went together to Neyasnaya Polyana.* A group of cheery children tagged along behind us: Lenochka Treneva, Varya Arbuzova, Lenya Pasternak and some others—a happy garland of six-, five-, and eight-year-olds—with them a fight's not a fight, a game's not a game. They roll about, squeal, grab each other in a kind of broad rhythm, which seems to come naturally to children on a sunny fall day— they gave me sunflowers, stripped an entire rowan tree of its berries for me—and out of a terrible funereal melancholy I suddenly became so merry, so openly, boundlessly, childishly merry, that Al(exei) Iv(anovich) must have been astonished at such a fit of friskiness in an old man.

I entered the isolation ward to see the children there. . .I sat with the sick children over an hour, quietly telling them stories— and my sense of banality left me. . .Yesterday before the rain I went to the barber to get a shave. There was a line. I had to wait a long time. I waited in a garden with several oaktrees. Three girls, Nina, Lida, and someone else, were playing ball. I began to play with them, showed them all the games I knew, and lost my place in the barbershop line. An old man's childishness, but I remember those two hours as the best I had in Kiev.

It was, I think, the fifth of October. The weather was wonderful and dry. Students from School No. 589 came to visit me, the fifth grade and the second grade. I'd had a headache, had been lying down in a somber frame of mind—and suddenly all these marvelous, happy, indefatigable children. I spent four hours with them

---

*A playful neighborhood name for the street in Peredelkino where Pasternak lived, an allusion to Tolstoy's Yasnaya Polyana. (Translator)

and got well again. I didn't feel even the slightest bit tired. They gathered wood for a campfire, ran races, filled our woods with hubbub, laughter, shouts—it seems to me I've never been as much in love with any woman as with these bright-eyed friends. All of them at once. They seemed much better than our (petty bourgeois) Peredelkino children. I read them a lot of my stories in the libr(ary)—they listened attentively. Then they ran along the benches, showed off gymnastics exercises, climbed trees, the girls no less well than the boys.

I wasn't the one looking after him that day in Peredelkino. Kornei Ivanovich had suffered a heart spasm not long before; the doctors had said he could get up but shouldn't get overtired. And then these schoolchildren arrived. Kornei Ivanovich read out loud to them, then raising his voice, directed them in races around the garden. A boy began to climb a tree. Standing near the trunk, the teacher yelled: "Lipatov, climb down! Get down this instant! Do you hear me! Lipatov!"

Kornei Ivanovich stood at the base of the same tree. At the top of his still-youthful voice, he cried: "Climb higher, higher, Volodya! There's a good, wide branch, see it? Climb, don't look down."

I thought he was too excited, had been outdoors too long, was straining his voice and taxing his heart. "Kornei Ivanovich is tired," I said quietly to the teacher. "He should go in now."

He overheard me. "Don't listen to that old biddy!" he shouted angrily. "I'm not a bit tired! I'm feeling fine! Okay, children, who can collect the most pine cones?"

He had recently turned seventy-eight. Yet that day I, the "old biddy," recalled with piercing clarity our games at Kuokkala, and the way he'd taught Kolya and me to climb trees.

What did his friendships with children provide? Subject matter for observation? Not only that.

> . . .my sense of banality somehow left me.
> . . .I suddenly became so merry, so openly, boundlessly, childishly merry . . .
> Strange that I can only relax when I'm with children . . .
> . . .I . . .showed them all the games I knew . . .and I remember those two hours as the best I spent in Kiev.
> . . .I read them a lot of my stories—they listened attentively.

So, contact with children cured him of melancholy; it wasn't just that it didn't tire him, it actively renewed him; it cleansed him of banality (it is as rare for children to be banal, as it is common for adults to be so). He loved to read children prose and poetry; children, he believed, are more sensitive to art than anyone else and make the most creative audiences. Children combined everything by which he lived: heightened sensitivity to art and nature, and a creative approach to life.

> . . . I never was as much in love with any woman as I was with these bright-eyed friends. All of them at once.

He fell in love with those schoolchildren who so happily climbed trees and then listened to his reading—as we had once climbed trees and listened to his reading, only not in the woods, but by the sea.

Then suddenly amidst his diary entries comes one which is most unusual for him, unlike all the others, as though it were written not by that old man who became "openly" and "boundlessly merry" among children, but by a different old man, or rather an elder—great, gloomy, immortal, as if that elder,* taking up arms against art in an angry sermon about goodness, separating art forcefully from the service of good, had dictated these lines to him:

> . . . I really ought to abandon literature all together—and devote myself to children—read to them, tell them stories, stimulate them, inspire them to a worthy, humane life; without that, simply dispensing books is useless.

These lines appeared once and were never repeated. Certainly, he always realized that distributing books at his Library was not enough in and of itself, and therefore twice a year he organized "Campfire" performances featuring actors, acrobats and poets, and regularly asked accomplished acquaintances of his from different professions to come to the library to talk to children.

He did all this both before and after he wrote that odd diary entry. But "abandon literature all together," in other words, all his own literary work, and devote himself entirely to children, as he writes here—that he could not have done. He would never have been capable of such self-denial. Literature, art, books, his own and other people's, were throughout his life dearer to him than anything else. And no matter how great his devotion to children, he was totally absorbed in his literary work.

In the 1910's, in the long-ago Kuokkala period, he was one of the best known and widely read critics in Russia. Nothing could have separated him from his work as a critic at that time, not even his interest in children. And

---

*An allusion to Tolstoy. (Translator)

he always looked for signs of artistic talent in children before anything else, or at least valued their tribe as, of all the tribes of humanity, the most sensitive to art. He thought of himself as a natural-born critic, an instrument created to respond to art, and in fact he was such an instrument, responding as it were to poetry and prose, both classical and modern, not only with eye and ear, but with the tips of his fingers and every inch of skin. He was a fanatic about literary work. He was obsessed by art.

In the course of his long life, he wrote, translated, and edited thousands of pages. Philology, the history of literature, textology, memoir, commentary. Literary portraits, critical articles.

"I have rarely met a man," wrote Ilya Efimovich Repin about him to Anatoly Fedorovich Koni in 1914, "so deserving of books...His phenomenal love for literature, deep respect for manuscripts inspires us all..."[1]

During the war, when he was already established as a famous storyteller, he wrote to a friend from evacuation: "I understood (maybe too late) that the foundation of my calling is description, literary portraits, and I was happy working on them."

He was a critic, an appraiser of art, by vocation. He was born to it.

On 28 October 1968, a year before his death, he wrote to me when he was working on his collected works and rereading the criticism he wrote in the 1910s and 1920s: "I'm immersed in my seventh volume: my best articles will appear in this volume.* Oh my, my writing went pretty well once upon a time, and I never suspected it. There wasn't one day when I was satisfied with myself and my work, and only now, a thousand years later, can I see how conscientiously and diligently I worked."

He could have described his own devotion to literary work in the words of Repin. Nothing's precisely comparable here except one thing: the lifelong commitment to art. For both men the foundation of existence was artistic work.

"...I love art...more than any other human happiness and joy," wrote Repin. "I love it secretly, jealously, incurably, like an old drunk...No matter where I am, what I'm involved in, no matter who may delight me, nor what may attract me...Anywhere and everywhere, art is in my mind, my heart and my best, most treasured wishes. The morning hours, which I dedicate to it, are the best hours of my existence. And the joys and the sorrows which I experience in these hours—joy unto bliss, and sorrow unto death—with their rays brighten or darken every event in my life."[2]

Yes, Kornei Ivanovich loved children and gave much of himself to them. He also gained much from them—spontaneous happiness and "angries" and "smeareline"**. However, art was what gave his life meaning. He loved

---

*Though prepared, this volume was never published. (Translator)

**Serditki, angry wrinkles, and mazeline, vaseline, examples of children's speech from From Two to Five. (Translator)

children primarily for their creative approach to the world—their sensitivity to nature, play and poetry. For the fact that they, like small gods, created words.

"One must respect the soul of the child," he wrote in his article "On Children's Language," "it is the spirit of the creator and the artist."[3]

Kornei Chukovsky, the critic, was also an artist. Without understanding this, one cannot understand either the design of his critical articles or the reasons for their influence. He worked on his articles the way other people work on poetry, composed his paragraphs like verses, subjecting his thoughts and examples to a rhythm—hidden but inherent in any prose—assaying the weight, age, and sound of every word, listening to how it sounded with the words next to it; he wrote to be read aloud. His articles (no less than his tales in verse) were intended to be read in a strong voice in an auditorium full of people who, hearing them, were not for one minute to grow bored, yawn, or whisper to their neighbor.

This is the reason for the variety of internal gestures expressed in a variety of intonations, the sharp and unexpected turns of thought—all were intended for the listener, although the articles were written for newspaper column and printed page.

"I finished writing the lecture on the train,"[4] he reported on one trip through provincial towns.

"Finished writing the lecture," that is, something appropriate for reading aloud.

Many people, particularly poets, appreciated the "singing," sonorous quality of his articles, the rhythmic way he expressed his thoughts. The poetess Olga Dyachkova, having heard Kornei Ivanovich lecture in seminars at "World Literature" and "The House of Art," wrote the following lines (a portrait of him, of his lecture-articles, and of his manner of lecturing):

> Less boredom on the most bored faces lingers.
> He comes. Another cubit-length of stride—
> And on the table his big hands, long fingers,
> Round big, impressive papers now reside.
> And with a gratifying, cordial presentation
> He strokes the audience, as if a soft, warm thing,
> And like a diva, loving demonstration,
> His article triumphantly does *sing*.[5]

You can only sing something which has rhythm.

You don't sing a certificate or a report.

It was customary in the past, and it is customary now, to call Chukovsky's criticism, particularly his early articles, subjective.

The charge is just: his articles are as subjective as any lyric poem.

The charge is unjust: they are as subjective in their extreme originality of

133

opinion and style as was the extremely original voice which expressed them. However, like any artist, Kornei Chukovsky tried (if in his own, subjective way) to express a judgment that was objective. How far he succeeded in this is another question. I only want to emphasize that it is important to measure his articles by the standards we apply to art, not by the elementary idea of "right or wrong" which is usually applied to criticism. For example, his article on Leonid Andreev is no less an artistic creation than the short stories of Andreev which he is analyzing, or more accurately, depicting. Though he did not have a high opinion of his own gifts, he did consider himself an artist when he was working.

Characteristic in this regard are comments he made in several letters.

Insisting that Tamara Grigoryevna Gabbe, in collaboration with friends, should write a history of literature for children, he suggested—in 1939—that she write portraits of the writers Panteleev, Zhitkov, Ilyin, Barto, Vvedensky, Kharms, Paustovsky, Kataev, and Zoshchenko, and felt it essential to warn her "not to be afraid of impressionism" since the articles were to be provided with a scholarly apparatus.

" . . . the scholarly apparatus will serve as a compensation for the reader. It will offset those elements *appearing to smack of dilettantism*, which are an integral part of any impressionistic description."[6]

What's important here is what he reveals about himself. Kornei Chukovsky's articles are impressionistic, but the basis for impressionistic articles is study and scholarship.

In 1920 in a letter to Gorky[7] defining his critical method, Kornei Chukovsky clearly stated that the critic is obliged to both artist and scholar:

> I study a writer's favorite devices, his bias for one or another epithet, trope, figure, rhythm, word, and on the basis of this strictly formal, technical, scientific analysis I draw psychological conclusions, reconstruct the spiritual nature of the writer... Our dear 'Russian boys'* . . . insist upon formal method, demand that numbers, weights and measures be applied to literary work, but they stop there; I think it's necessary to go further, that on the basis of the formal study of the material, it's necessary to reconstruct what used to be called the soul of the poet. . . Criticism ought to be universal, scholarly discoveries ought to lead to emotion. Critical analysis ought to culminate in synthesis: while the critic analyzes, he's a scholar, but when he turns to synthesis, he's an artist, creating an artistic image of a man from small and accidentally observed details.

---

*A reference to the Russian formalist critics. (Translator)

At the end of his life Kornei Chukovsky was awarded a doctor's degree in philology.* That was quite natural: he was a scholar. But he "created an artistic image of a man"—he was an artist. The techniques he used in his critical articles were the techniques of the artist. Whether his work was weak or strong is a different question, but without this key it won't yield to definition. Future researchers will study the stylistic qualities of his articles, as they already study the stylistics of his tales in verse. Kornei Chukovsky will inevitably attract his own Kornei Chukovsky. And that person, I believe, will study first of all the devices which reached two audiences. The critic must speak so that he can be understood not only by the refined reader, but also "the callow student, and the young secretary in the commissar's office," as Kornei Ivanovich declared in his letter to Gorky.

A critical article, therefore, is a message addressed to two audiences. It can only reach both if the critic has the gifts of an artist.

Kornei Chukovsky, critic and feuilletonist, possessed this gift.

"Abandon literature!"—that he could never have done.

His "joy unto bliss, and sorrow unto death" all occurred when he was writing.

"What a struggle with style and composition," he admitted in 1923, "and much else which critics usually don't bother with! Every critical article I write is a work of art (perhaps bad, but art!) and when I wrote my article 'Nat Pinkerton,' for ex(ample), it seemed to me I was writing a poem."[8]

(Indicative of these efforts is his choice of titles: *Critical Stories, Tales of Nekrasov,* and *Portraits of Contemporary Writers.* And here's a new characterization: turns out he considered his articles narrative poems.)

I remember, one winter, in Kuokkala, when he was buried in one of his latest "poems," he fled his warmly heated dacha, his convenient desk, for someone else's empty, unlived in, frozen, roughhewn shed, and for hours, days at a time, wrote there without a desk, sitting on the floor on a newspaper in his overcoat, felt boots and fur hat, huddled against the wall. Alone, totally isolated from other people. It was probably just then he felt he was writing a poem. In his hands a pencil and a board holding his paper, which he rests on his sharp-pointed knees. Scattered all around him on the floor, books and used sheets of paper. Vapor rises from his lips.

Honoris Causa by Oxford University. (Translator)

CHAPTER

XVII

However, now we've returned there, it is time to take leave of Kuokkala.

In the spring of 1917, sometime after February,* Kornei Ivanovich and his family moved to Petrograd—at first to a tiny apartment on the corner of Leshtukov Lane and Zagorodny Prospect, and then (in 1919) into the big, spacious apartment at No. 6 Manezhny Lane, where he lived for almost twenty years, until he moved to Moscow in 1938.

I don't remember exactly which month in 1917 he moved us from Kuokkala to Petrograd. I know only that from September 1917 Kolya and I went to school on Mokhovaya Street: Kolya at the Tenishev School (right across the street from the building where, as I remember, the publishing house "World Literature" was later located), I, at the Tagantseva Gymnasium (on the corner of Mokhovaya and Panteleymonovskaya). Soon both these institutions were merged to become Comprehensive School No. 15; Kolya and I were in different grades, but under one roof and often ran across the street together to Kornei Ivanovich... Soon Boba, too, began to study at this same school.

"My children were fortunate"—our good fortune followed us: at "World Literature," at the "House of the Literati," at "The House of Art," and in our own home, we saw Blok, Akhmatova, Gorky, Mandelstam, Kuzmin, Khodasevich, Gumilyov, Zamyatin, Zoshchenko, Babel, and many, many others.

Once again we saw and listened to Mayakovsky.

Kuokkala ended forever for Kornei Ivanovich sooner than for me. I was there in 1940 and then again at the beginning of the sixties. He went there for the last time in 1925—to see Repin.

In the sixties I walked along those same stones where Kolya had done his dreaming, looked at the brook where Kornei Ivanovich with our help had

---

*i.e., after the revolution of February 1917. (Translator)

once built dams, passed through the sparse pines and entered the house. On the outside it looked much as it had when we'd lived there; inside it was all redone, only the heating stoves were the same, and his study, and the stairway to the second floor, which I'd once run down so carefully, afraid the stairs would creak.

The name of the station stop had already been changed to Repino. Penates had become a museum. I couldn't bring myself to open the gate into Repin's park: if I took a look at the well where we'd drawn water as children, I might suddenly hear:

> Two stumps,
> Two root clumps...
> Mustn't let the pail be splashed...

When, upon my return, I described to Kornei Ivanovich my recent excursion from the Writers' Colony at Komarovo to Repino, he listened gloomily, as if not paying attention. He asked not a single question. I said no more.

The memory of how he'd lost the Kuokkala dacha and it had come to be plundered was not a happy one for him. On the sea of life he'd been just as careless and casual as on the real sea, that day when he'd nearly drowned himself and us.

In 1922 when we were already living in Petrograd, not Kuokkala, Kornei Ivanovich gave temporary permission to live in the dacha to the former husband of an artist who'd been a Kuokkala neighbor (like Kornei Ivanovich, a visitor to Penates). He had complained that he had no place to live, and Kornei Ivanovich had given him the required written permission. The onetime husband of our onetime neighbor proved to be a full-time rascal. After our departure, the dacha had remained untouched for several years, full of furniture and books: when our parents had left for Petrograd in the spring of 1917, they had planned to return that summer and therefore had taken only the most essential things with them.

Our neighbors had kept watch over the house. But seeing the owner's handwritten note of permission, they allowed the lodger to move in. He repaid Kornei Ivanovich handsomely for his unfounded trust: he sold all the most valuable furniture, household utensils, and books. And fled. In his wake came other robbers who completed the devastation.

"Everybody here knows and remembers you," wrote Repin to Kornei Ivanovich from Kuokkala in the summer of 1923. "Just yesterday on my way to Ollila, I looked sadly at your darkened house, at the overgrown yard and paths, remembering the continuous ebb and flow of all kinds of young literature which had taken place there! Especially the futurists...and Alexsei Tolstoy, and Boris Sadovskoy...Later, I was griefstricken to see a great multitude of ripped brochures on the floor, covered with muddy bootprints, between the ragged, once-elegant sofas where we used to spend such fascinating and comfortable hours listening to interesting lectures and lively discussions by talented writers, fanned by the bright flame of freedom. Why, a veritable platform of rare and valuable books and manuscripts lay on the floor of the library, and beneath this thick layer, glass crunched and cracked unbearably."

Imagine how unbearable the sound of glass crunching underfoot on the platform of books must have been to the owner, entering his former house.

In 1925, in January, Kornei Ivanovich went to Helsinki and then to Kuokkala, to visit Repin at Penates and to see his dacha.

This is the entry in his diary: "I do not love things; I'm not the least bit sorry about the stolen bureau, cupboard, lamps or mirrors, but I care a great deal about *the part of myself preserved in those things.*"

Yes, a person, particularly an important one, is imprinted in his things: the home he created is also he, his likeness; a mask, a mold, but one made from his living, working spirit, not from his dead face.

"I love the part of myself preserved in those things..."

Things, like a sponge absorbing water, can absorb and preserve time past. The loss of his things was the loss of the beloved time with which they were imprinted. The lamp which the thief had stolen from his house and sold had stood upon the bureau and cast its light upon him when he was not yet thirty, when his children were little, when he lived right on the sea catercorner to Penates, when from early spring to late autumn he went barefoot on the sand, along the Big Road and in the woods; when Mayakovsky read him "Cloud in Trousers," and he went to Repin's to read Pushkin out loud to him, or a lecture on contemporary literature to Repin and his guests in the gazebo; when in 1916, during the war, he prepared for a return trip to England, no longer the unknown boy correspondent of 1903, but as a member of a delegation of Russian journalists and writers; when so many marvelous people—poets, scientists, artists—gathered at Repin's house on Wednesdays and at his house on Sundays; when he wrote his lecture-poems on Fedor Sologub, Leonid Andreev, Korolenko, on Lydia Charskaya, on the futurists; when with his "lectures" he traveled all over Russia.

The lamp had been a piece of his life, a part of his existence.

"I do not love things."—"I care deeply about the part of myself preserved in those things."

(Today, for me, the essence of his existence is "preserved" in his Peredelkino house in *The Encyclopedia Britannica*, which accompanied him through his whole life, from young manhood on, and in the copy of the Repin portrait done in 1910. He never parted with those things and removed them in time from Kuokkala.)

"...I am alone, welcoming the New Year with a pen in my hand," wrote Kornei Ivanovich in Petrograd in 1923, "but I am not unhappy: my pen is very precious to me—my lamp, my inkwell—and here on the desk is my dear *Encyclopedia Britannica*, which I love so fondly. What a lot of knowledge she has given me, how soothing and affectionate she is."

Now when I pass the shelves holding the green volumes of *The Encyclopedia*, I cannot lift my eyes.

I want to touch them, caress their green covers, but I cannot.

I feel envious and uncomfortable when some member of the household, naturally and without thinking about it, takes one of the green books from the shelf and rustles through the pages, looking for information. Kornéi Ivanovich would certainly be happy to know that *The Encyclopedia* is still in service, that it does not occupy its shelves in vain, continuing to teach others. But myself I cannot touch it.

For me it represents both Kuokkala and the green mound of his grave.

There is one image of him which is clearer to me than any other: he snatches from the shelf the volume he needs—in Kuokkala, Petrograd, Moscow, or Peredelkino; his long, flexible, always suntanned, immaculately clean fingers leaf through the book; his eyes seek, they find. With a huge hand he smooths a glossy map: seems this city is all split up by rivers! Ah, I didn't know that! Or, it seems that philosopher produced his major work in 1897! And I, ignoramus, thought somehow it was 1891! Then clapping the book shut, he gratefully and gently returns it to its place.

He might be young as he was in Kuokkala, or he might be in his eighties.

He probably loved *The Encyclopedia Britannica* as much as the pen with which he wrote. "What a lot of knowledge she has given me, how soothing and affectionate she is."

For me his glance is forever lodged there, soundlessly seeking some map, someone's history, soundlessly calling to me from these books.

The photograph of the Repin portrait, inscribed by Repin, which accompanied Kornei Ivanovich on his moves, also remains a permanent memorial to the Kuokkala period: the friendship with artistic people, the "co-Kuokkalaship," as Sergeev-Tsensky called that time.

To the end of his days Repin fondly remembered his "co-Kuokkalaship" with Kornei Ivanovich.

"...passing Scherezade,* I recall your tall, merry figure," he wrote to Chukovsky in 1923, "do you remember how you lifted the trees knocked over by a storm? We had a big storm not long ago, but Scherezade still *stands*; only the paths are frightfully overgrown with grass from disuse (Emelyan mowed them yesterday, otherwise it would have been impossible to use them, especially in the morning—with the dew. And I go barefoot. And I always think of you.) You're a fiery person, may God keep you healthy ...Do you remember how at our outdoor gatherings in the park for the local people you offered tea—inexpensively—to our proletarian public. A cup

---

*Scherezade, Kiosk, and the Temple of Isida were all gazebos at Penates. (Author)

of tea cost one kopeck; cookies, one kopeck. How the women and girls loved you. Yes, you were always the center of attention, inspiring courage and freedom. Do you remember the lectures? The readings by Mayakovsky, S. Gorodetsky, Gorky, the singing of Skitalets and others (in the Kiosk), but not in the Temple of Isida, where Tarkhanov, Leonid Andreev and A. Svirsky were reading."[1]

In 1925 more about "co-Kuokkalaship": "Yes, if you were living here, I would fly to you every free minute: we share so many common interests. But most of all, you are inexhaustible... You react to everything and know so very, very much; my conversation with you is—always—*headlong*—worthwhile."[2]

Ilya Efimovich especially loved the way Kornei Ivanovich read, his voice. In his letters he called that voice "swanlike," "like an angel's," "inspiring of delight;" and his readings, "solo concerts." The Repin portrait of Chukovsky was mute, like all other portraits. But the turn of the head, the posture, the fingers embracing a book—all the paint and every line—seem to me to convey not only his appearance (a young, dark-haired man with a small black moustache and a book in his hand), but also the magic of his penetrating, ringing, singsong voice.

In 1923, in answer to his detailed letter about Kuokkala, Chukovsky wrote Repin: "Kuokkala is my homeland, my childhood..."

"Childhood"... the beginning of beginnings. Many things began for him there, in Kuokkala. Many things which developed and reached their conclusion only at the end of his life. (What he is speaking of here is his spiritual homeland, his spiritual childhood.)

And for me, that is where he began, that is where my childhood began and ended, but he did not end there.

In Kuokkala he began to create the genre and style of his artistic work, his articles, lectures, "critical stories," essays, portraits, reasearch—the style of the very diverse work of Kornei Chukovsky.

In Kuokkala he became acquainted with, became friends with, and entered into regular contact with dozens of people from the literary and artistic world—contacts which continued from that time forward. This is where *Chukokkala* began. This is where he began to study the psychology of young children, leading to *From Two to Five*. The "Campfires," flaring up later to the tallest of the tall pinetrees, every year in Peredelkino, also had their beginning here. And the children's plays in which children acted but the sets and costumes were designed by professional artists were also the fruits of Kuokkala.

(In the Kornei Chukovsky archive there exists to this day a public announcement, written in his hand; it advertises a children's pageant featuring artists, performers, musicians; the play *The Pot-bellied Tsar*, acted by children; all the proceeds from this pageant—according to the announcement—will go towards the purchase of books for a children's library . . . That was the summer of 1916; he built the library forty-one years later, in the fall of 1957.)

The dream of a library linking writers, artists, performers, children and books was fulfilled in Peredelkino, but it was born in Kuokkala.

How often he was distracted from it! And how often he returned to it! I can remember how he raised and donated money to buy books for children, collected and donated books, when he was on vacation in Peterhof near Leningrad. Then in Luga. Then in Sestroretsk.

(That was the nature of his cheerful, restless, inconstant, and at the same time stubborn, natural, lifelong constancy.)

Here in Kuokkala, between 1915 and 1916, *Crocodile* was written—Kornei Chukovsky's first book for children. Here's where he began other works which later grew into books: *Chekhov, Tales of Nekrasov, Contemporaries*, not to mention the fact that it was in Kuokkala that all his later work on Nekrasov, textology and literary annotation had its beginning.

He worked well back there in Kuokkala . . .

" . . . and the air is clean, . . . and the snow lies smoothly round about, and skis, and no people, and pine trees—sometimes I envy myself," wrote Kornei Ivanovich upon moving to Kuokkala.

There he discovered his spiritual homeland.

There I spent my childhood.

Afterword

[Only the first four chapters of *To the Memory of Childhood* have been published in the Soviet Union. Lydia Chukovskaya describes the circumstances of its writing and the problems with its publication in her book *The Process of Expulsion*, which documents her expulsion from the Union of Soviet Writers in 1974 for her support of dissident writers. This excerpt was translated from the Russian edition published in France in 1979 by YMCA-Press.]

My father died in October 1969. I am not going to write about my loss. I will only describe the action mounted against me by the Writers' Union immediately after the death of Kornei Ivanovich.

By this time I had served as a member of six Literary Heritage Commissions—commissions formed by the Union whenever a literary figure dies. I had served on the Literary Heritage Commission for Anna Akhmatova, N. P. Antsyferov, F. Vigdorova, T. Gabbe, Boris Zhitkov, and M. Ilyin.

But I was not included in the Literary Heritage Commission for Kornei Chukovsky.

Realistically, practically, in this specific instance, my "not-being-included" was meaningless. I had been close to my father and lived under the same roof with him not only in my childhood and youth, but also for many of the following decades. My memory was fully mobilized. "All that's mine, I carry with me." But the Union's insulting maneuver clearly demonstrates: a) the nature of their goal (separation, excommunication) and b) the moral level of those who invented the action. Execution over the fresh grave! Not everyone's capable of sinking so low.

Incidentally, any low deed can be matched by another even lower. It's possible to sink further, further, further still. With or without a goal, the pit of immorality into which the faller sinks is bottomless.

The goal quickly became clear.

In the last days of his life, in his hospital room, as was his wont, Kornei Ivanovich continued to work. He was working on an article, "Confessions of an Old Storyteller." The article was intended for the newspaper *Literary Russia*. About two weeks after his funeral, with the help of friends, I managed to piece the article together from his rough drafts and outlines and prepare it for publication. I sent it to the editors. After a month or so I noticed that Kornei Chukovsky's article had not yet appeared in *Literary Russia*.

Ordinarily it was the newspaper most eager, most insistent to have his work.

I asked someone to telephone and find out what had happened.

The answer from Comrade Pozdnyaev, the editor-in-chief, came back as follows: "We'd be glad to publish it...But, unfortunately, we can't... There's a note appended to it which reads: 'Prepared for publication by Lydia Chukovskaya.' "

I asked that Comrade Pozdnyaev be informed that I was more than willing to retract the subversive tag line. Provided they printed the article.

(This was arithmetic in action; the subject, after all, was not a manuscript of mine, but someone else's. Take away, take away my infamous name! I agree—just so long as Kornei Chukovsky's posthumous article appears, in which a critic analyzes a poet's verse, and the critic and the poet are one and the same person...A rare event, indeed, in literature: an author using the full panoply of his critical skills to analyze his own work.)

But my response didn't satisfy the newspaper.

Pozdnyaev: Lydia Chukovskaya's oral retraction is not enough. Let her submit her (!) wishes in writing.

I submitted them. With the greatest of pleasure. I wrote a letter to the newspaper and kept a copy. I love putting things in writing. What's written by the pen can't be cut out by the axe. Culture is the trail of the noble impulses of the human spirit, hardened and set, the tracks intersect, cross and lay down new roads to the future. Fearless memory preserves these tracks, defends them—sometimes from shallowness and indifference, sometimes from atrocity. But I think that even the tracks of atrocity must be preserved. (Otherwise people will not know that culture is not simply work, it is battle.) The telephone conversation with Pozdnyaev would have vanished into eternity, but the tracks of violence, petty vengeance, atrocity, engraved on paper—my letter of retraction to Pozdnyaev—is preserved. And someday it will offer itself as material for studying the literary mores of the seventies in Russia. I was allowed to prepare Kornei Chukovsky's article for publication. But to note: "Prepared for publication by Lydia Chukovskaya"—was not allowed.

I wrote: "Having learned that the article by my father which I prepared for publication, 'Confessions of an Old Storyteller,' has not appeared in your newspaper solely because of the reference to my name, I herewith state that I am willing to withdraw my name as its editor."

Once *Literary Russia* received my letter, they quickly published Kornei Ivanovich's last article.[1]

These humiliations did not keep me from continuing the work I'd begun earlier. On the contrary, they somehow stirred me to action. Since the fall of 1969, I'd had new projects, new work on my shoulders. Kornei Ivanovich's literary secretary and assistant of many years, Klara Israelevna Lozovskaya, along with old friends of ours and my daughter Elena, was organizing the archive, which covered the years from 1900 to 1969, a visible, concrete trail of Russian culture across almost two-thirds of a century; they were also inventorying and cataloging the five-thousand-volume library. I had begun to look over Kornei Ivanovich's letters, primarily those written to me—from 1912 to 1969. In addition, I proposed an idea to the other members of the family: that we not use those rooms in the Peredelkino dacha which Kornei Chukovsky had occupied for the last thirty years, but leave them as they were, without the slightest change. Three rooms out of five—the ones which, in appearance and appointments, most reflected his tastes, habits, skills and way of life. He was very photogenic, expressive in every word and gesture—his voice, his walk, his hands—this expressiveness is characteristic of his rooms as well; of his desk; his bookshelves, toys, pictures, photographs; even the benches and woods outside the windows, even the starling-house in the birch tree, where his favorite squirrels lived. This microworld, built up over thirty years, reflects his personality every bit as much as each of his articles, photographs or recordings of his voice. Kornei Ivanovich was by nature hard-working and sociable—the spirit of concentrated work and cheerful, varied, energetic association with people lives on in his rooms. These aren't just the traces of his own personality, but of Russian culture. How many poets, old and young, how many linguists, philologists, translators, how many experts in English and American literature climbed those stairs! How many books and letters were read and written in that study and at that desk; on the balcony or in the woods! (He'd rest his piece of paper on a board.) How many voices reading aloud great poetry and great prose were heard within these walls, and how many parodies and jokes!

On 5 October 1969, Kornei Ivanovich left his house for the hospital—I asked the family to leave his rooms exactly as they were when he descended the stairs for the last time. Not to use them. To leave them—as a memorial to him.

People don't learn right away not to touch things, not to move them from place to place, not to use familiar items. After all, just a moment ago everything was in motion.

Little by little we learned.

But there was one more thing I had to do: write my reminiscences of him. After all, there aren't many people still alive who remember him as a young man. He'd had four children. I am the sole survivor. I remember our childhood and his young years. It was up to me to write.

I set to work on my reminiscences. I conceived of them in three parts, but felt I must write first of all about the time almost no one else could recall: Kornei Chukovsky's life in Finland, in Kuokkala (now the village of Repino), between 1912 and 1917.

I wrote the first, pre-revolutionary Kuokkala part in 1970–71. It was intended for a collection of articles in memory of Kornei Chukovsky to be put out by Detgiz*. My piece was therefore entitled: "To the Memory of my Father." The compilers of the collection informed me that the editorial board of Detgiz had greeted my memoir with pleasure. I did not fear problems with the censor: the first part dealt with the years before the revolution and mostly with Kornei Ivanovich's games with small children. How he taught us to row a clumsy fisherman's boat; how he taught us English; how together we carried water from Repin's well; how he recited to us out at sea the poetry of Baratynsky, Nekrasov, Tyutchev. The action takes place before 1917; I am very young, between the ages of five and ten; too young to be politically responsible, not at all dangerous; and I have something to write about (all those well-known names!): with my own unsophisticated eyes I see Repin, Korolenko, Leonid Andreev, Mayakovsky, Chaliapin...

(And the Kuokkala dacha, though empty, is extant; it has not yet collapsed, it still stands**; it also remembers their steps and voices; it is still possible to save this small knot of Russian culture, woven of so many different threads...In addition to the people I mentioned above, others who visited there were N. Gumilyov, and Anna Akhmatova, and N. Evreinov, and N. Kulbin, and Boris Grigoriev, and Boris Sadovskoy, and Teffi, and Shklovsky, and Ivan Puni.)

After the *Literary Russia* episode I, of course, no longer offered any of my work to any magazine or newspaper publisher. Comrade Pozdnyaev had spelled out the situation for me in no uncertain terms. Upon receiving the letter he'd required, in which I myself asked him to remove the words "Prepared for publication by Lydia Chukovskaya," he said something even more instructive: "My conscience as a communist does not allow me to print the name Lydia Chukovskaya in my newspaper. No one in authority has told me not to, I myself consider it impossible." In other words, what was at work was not the conscience of the party as a whole, but the personal communist conscience of Comrade Pozdnyaev.

However, it was soon evident how far that which motivated Comrade

---

*Children's State Publishing House. (Translator)
**Unfortunately the Kuokkala dacha has since burned down. (Translator)

Pozdnyaev (I don't know if one can call it conscience) had been deprived of its unique and individual nature.

But first something quite magical, improbable, and unprecedented occurred. The magazine *Family and School* expressed interest in seeing my reminiscences of Kornei Ivanovich. Though I had no hopes whatsoever (after the silent demise of the Akhmatova book at the Leningrad publishers* and the eloquent explanations of Comrade Pozdnyaev), I agreed to let *Family and School* magazine see my reminiscences. The fairy tale which unfolded dazzled me. There were fifteen chapters in my memoir at the time. Lyubov Mikhailovna Ivanovna, the then editor of *Family and School*, telephoned me with such complimentary words about the artistic strength of my memoir I'm embarrassed to repeat them. Lyubov Mikhailovna Ivanovna suggested publishing all fifteen chapters in slightly abridged form. She thought they would be appropriate for parents, for teachers, and for children. Having lost my confidence, I stubbornly suggested publishing just one chapter, the one most important to me: the one which describes how Kornei Ivanovich recited poetry to us out on the sea. No, better all fifteen. No, I'd prefer just the one! No, better all fifteen. Thus we bargained and bargained and, finally, agreed on seven chapters. They were to appear in three issues of *Family and School* for 1972—Nos. 9, 10, and 11.

So here I am, unable to believe my eyes, holding issue No. 9 of the magazine—and there, indeed, is the first excerpt of my reminiscences published under the title "On the Seashore." The fairy tale is carried to the limit: not only does my subversive name, which Comrade Pozdnyaev's sensitive conscience forbade him to set in print, appear in large letters, not only does it say openly "Lydia Chukovskaya. On the Seashore," but at the end of the excerpt are the words: "To be continued" and there's even a picture of me! the Mayakovsky drawing, done in 1915.[2]

And Comrade Pozdnyaev's conscience had scarcely seemed a purely personal matter! Not really conscience so much as a directive from above.

The excerpt in issue No. 9 ended with the words: "To be continued."

The excerpt in No. 10, a few paragraphs from the next chapter, began with the words: "The end."

I felt very sorry for the editor-in-charge, Lyubov Mikhailovna: she promises an author to publish memoirs in three issues, then opens the magazine she herself has edited and instead of "to be continued," abruptly reads "the end." The change was made without her knowledge. I also felt sorry for Kornei Ivanovich: the excerpt describes how he taught us children to get down

---

*In 1967 Lydia Chukovskaya was asked to edit the first posthumous collection of Anna Akhmatova's work. The Leningrad publisher abruptly canceled the book without a word of explanation just as it was going to press. The incident is described in the previous chapter of *The Process of Expulsion*. (Translator)

on all fours and bark at a dog, but there's not a word about how he taught us to understand poetry. A famous writer, critic, memoirist, literary historian, philologist, expert in Russian poetry, a man concerned all his life about "the poetic education of children"; poet and author of numerous tales in verse; author of works on the theory of translation, master translator; in a word—Kornei Chukovsky, the famous writer and poetry lover, is turned into some kind of frivolous entertainer.

I still don't know whether this abrupt break occurred because somebody "at the top" in 1968 had decided that nothing of mine should be published, or because just then, in the summer of 1972, Chekhov Publishers had published my earlier novella *Going Under* (1953-57) in the west. And Voice of America, by discussing this book over the radio, had aroused the personal conscience of every newspaper and magazine editor in the Soviet Union.

"To the memory of my father" . . . He was not tormented in a labor camp, nor shot. In the last ten years of his life he enjoyed prosperity and fame. However, his life had its own tragedy and its own conflict. He was blessed with a rare gift: he was a talented literary critic, with a heightened sensitivity to verbal art. In the 1910s and early 1920s no important literary development occurred without comment from Kornei Chukovsky in his special, always distinctive voice. The best of his articles from that time are polemical, and sometimes even paradoxical—through external analysis of an author's style they lead the reader within, to the very core, to comprehension of the author's spiritual nature. The articles themselves are works of art, primarily of portraiture. By the end of the twenties, however, Chukovsky ceased being a literary critic. The times rendered originality of perception impossible in any field whatsoever—including literature, and the same went for originality in criticism. The government bureaucracy reduced the job of the literary critic to popularization of the latest "party resolutions in the area of literature." Kornei Chukovsky continued to work in his other specialties, but until the end of his life he keenly and painfully felt his failure to realize his principal vocation. . . For decades he took part in the battle to assure the child's right to fairy tales—both folk and literary—and came out of this battle victorious. Fairy tales—tales in general—were looked upon with suspicion by the authorities: the ignoramuses in positions of power felt that fairy tales kept children from understanding reality. Every one of Chukovsky's tales, which today are born anew with each new generation of children, have become folklore, and provided the language with numerous proverbs and sayings, each one of Kornei Chukovsky's tales—from *Crocodile* and *The Boldly Buzzing Fly* to *Bibigon*—in its time suffered persecution and the threat of censorship.

However, in my reminiscences I did not undertake to write about his struggles and his problems. I didn't write about his fight for the fairy tale, because he himself wrote about that in his book *From Two to Five*,[3] or about Chukovsky as a critic because I'm sure that others will remember and write about that as soon as this "secret heritage" is returned to the reader.

I set about recollecting in my reminiscences what I alone in all the world know about: my childhood and his youthful friendship with children.

But ours is a planned system: who is to remember whom, what is appropriate to root in memory, and what must be rooted out, who is to be denoted close to and who distant from Kornei Chukovsky is not for us to judge. The authorities know better.

It's been decided—I'm not to reminisce about him.

About the Author

Born in 1907 in St. Petersburg, Lydia Korneyevna Chukovskaya has observed or participated in most of the major literary events of Russia's tumultuous twentieth century. Her father was Kornei Ivanovich Chukovsky (1882–1969), the celebrated critic, editor, scholar, and children's author. A self-made intellectual, Kornei Chukovsky revered good writing, loved poetry, despised sham, and shared his convictions passionately with his children. His daughter took his lessons to heart, following them courageously throughout her career as editor, writer and human rights activist.

In a society which fears the truth, Lydia Chukovskaya has refused to lie. Such honesty has brought her into repeated conflict with the state. Her support for persecuted Soviet writers has cut her off from her own audience. Her writing and even her name were banned for years in the U.S.S.R., and she was expelled from the Soviet Union of Writers in 1974. Though unable to publish at home and cut off from normal contacts with her readers and editors abroad, she has continued to write and defend others' right to do so. *To the Memory of Childhood* (Pamiati Detstva), her loving chronicle of growing up beside the Gulf of Finland with her father, helps us to understand the sources of her strength and her belief in the power of the written word.

Kornei Chukovsky is a household name in the Soviet Union today because of his delightful tales in verse for children, which every Soviet child—and parent—knows and loves. His literary accomplishments, however, ranged far beyond the bedtime story. At the turn of the century he wrote controversial literary criticism and lively profiles of leading cultural figures. As a translator from English, he introduced such writers as Walt Whitman, Mark Twain, Rudyard Kipling, and Oscar Wilde to Russian readers. In the 1920s and 1930s he helped found a new literature for children and wrote *From Two to Five*, a book on children's language which has been reissued many times and translated into many languages. When his literature for children was attacked in the late thirties—Lenin's widow Krupskaya led the charge—he turned to scholarly study of the nineteenth century poet Nekrasov, extensive editing projects, and articles and books on the Russian language and the art of translation. A man of great energy and boundless appetite for work, Chukovsky played an active part in the cultural life of the country until he died at 87 in 1969.

Kornei Chukovsky introduced his own children to literature from their infancy, reciting poetry to them "on the ocean, at the teatable, on the road to the station." He told stories about writers who perished for telling the truth and spoke with scorn of the mediocre tyrants and bullies who persecuted them. His social circle included the major artists and writers of prerevolutionary Russia. Ilya Repin, the well-known painter, was a neighbor and friend. To Chukovsky's modest seaside home in Kuokkala (now Repino), a short train ride from St. Petersburg, came Chaliapin, Blok, Mayakovsky, Korolenko, Kuprin, and many others to share their ideas and their latest work. Because of their father, "art was in the very air" the Chukovsky children breathed.

The childhood idyll, but not the cultural exposure, came to an end when the family returned to the capital in 1917 at the time of the Revolution. Lydia and her brothers were educated at the former Tenishev School, one of the best in the city—among its earlier graduates were Osip Mandelstam and Vladimir Nabokov. With her father, she regularly attended readings by the important writers of the day, and the Chukovsky home remained a center of literary activity. After high school, Lydia Chukovskaya studied literature at the Institute of the History of Art, but her "real university" was her first job. She joined the staff of Samuil Ya. Marshak, a gifted editor and poet and friend of her father, who had recently founded the children's literature section of the Leningrad State Publishing House. Marshak set high standards for his writers and editors, and the books produced by the new department quickly became classics.

Rewarding literary work helped stave off the poverty and hunger of the postrevolutionary years, but nothing could stave off Stalin's terror once it began in the late 1930s. Most of Chukovskaya's co-workers and close friends were arrested, and Marshak's children's literature section was closed down for "bourgeois leanings." Chukovskaya's husband, astrophysicist and science writer Matvei Petrovich Bronshtein, was imprisoned and killed under torture. Chukovskaya herself narrowly escaped arrest.

In the winter of 1939–40, after two fruitless years of standing in line outside Leningrad's prisons for news of her husband, Chukovskaya wrote a novella describing the ordeal of a simple woman victimized by Stalin's purges. In those years committing such ideas to paper was a capital offense, and *Sofia Petrovna* is the only book of its kind written during those dreadful years. Jotted in a school notebook and hidden by a friend, it miraculously survived. In 1962 after Khrushchev had denounced Stalin and rehabilitated many of his victims and Solzhenitsyn's *One Day in the Life of Ivan Deni-*

sovich had appeared in print, *Sofia Petrovna* was accepted for publication. Young editors read it and wept, officious party hacks praised its truthfulness. Then, without warning, the book was canceled; the state had had enough truth about Stalin's crimes. Already in galley form, *Sofia Petrovna* passed from hand to hand, becoming one of the first samizdat publications in the Soviet Union. In 1965 it reached the West, where it was published under the title *The Deserted House* (Opustelyi dom). Though changes were made in the text without the author's permission, the book was hailed as the first to depict the corrosive effect of the Terror on everyday people, and it was translated into many languages.

Millions of Soviets shared Sofia Petrovna's experience of waiting in prison lines for news of loved ones; among them was the poet Anna Akhmatova, whose son Lev Gumilyov had been arrested in 1938. During this bitter year Chukovskaya and Akhmatova became close friends. Chukovskaya visited the poet regularly and from the first day kept a journal of their meetings, often in ciphered form. Drawing on her childhood training, Chukovskaya also memorized hundreds of lines of Akhmatova's poetry so they would not be lost. Akhmatova carefully wrote out verses on small scraps of paper for her friend to learn, then burnt the paper. To the regime, poetry was as dangerous as *Sofia Petrovna*.

When Germany attacked the Soviet Union in 1941, Chukovskaya was evacuated along with her daughter and her nephew to the East—first to Chistopol and then to Tashkent. In Chistopol, by chance, Chukovskaya met the poet Marina Tsvetaeva just before her suicide. She recorded her impressions in her diary, and this led, forty years later in 1981, to her vivid account of the poet's last desperate days. In Tashkent Chukovskaya worked with children in evacuation, trying to locate their parents or find them foster homes. The bravery of these young victims of the war touched Chukovskaya deeply, and she collected and edited a number of their stories in *Let the Children Have the Floor* (Slovo predostavliaetsia detiam, Tashkent, 1942).

Akhmatova joined Chukovskaya in Chistopol and moved with her to Tashkent. Their friendship and Chukovskaya's journals of their conversations continued until the poet's death in 1966 and became the basis for Chukovskaya's *Diary Notes on Anna Akhmatova* (Zapiski ob Anne Akhmatovoi), Volumes I and II. Published in the West in the 1970s and already translated into most major languages, these books provide an extraordinary record of the poet's life and of the cultural life of the nation over three decades. Chukovskaya is working on the third and final volume of the *Notes*.

After the war Lydia Chukovskaya was able once again to work as a writer and editor with Literaturnoe Nasledstvo (Literary Heritage) and other publishers. This experience and her earlier work with Marshak inspired numerous articles and a popular book, *In the Editor's Workshop* (V laboratorii redaktora, 1960, 1963), in which she analyzed the requirements of good editing. She warned against arbitrary censorship and exhorted writers to avoid dull, formulaic language, criticizing, in particular, the propagandistic children's books of the 1950s. Other of Chukovskaya's postwar literary projects reflect her admiration for the brave heroes of Russian history and literature whose stories Kornei Chukovsky recounted during the long Kuokkala winters. She wrote introductions for the *Collected Works of Taras Shevchenko* (1946), the martyred Ukrainian poet-hero, and for *Travels* (1947), the selected diaries and essays of Nikolai Miklukho-Maklai, the Russian explorer of the South Pacific. Her study of the artist-exile ethnographer, Nikolai Bestuzhev, resulted in *The Decembrists as Explorers of Siberia* (Dekabristy-issledovateli Sibiri, 1951), and her *Boris Zhitkov: A Critico-Biographical Essay* (Boris Zhitkov: Kritikobigraficheski ocherk, 1955) rekindled interest in long-neglected stories for adolescents by her father's childhood friend. The last of her books to be published in the Soviet Union was an appreciation of Alexander Herzen's historical memoir *My Past and Thoughts* (Byloe i dumy, Gertsena, 1966).

Along with Herzen, the nineteenth-century philosopher of revolution, she had come to understand that "silence supports despotism," and she began increasingly to speak out. In 1958 when Boris Pasternak received the Nobel prize for literature, he was vilified, expelled from the Writers' Union, and forced to renounce the award. Plain clothes agents in black cars followed him everywhere. Former friends turned on him; would-be supporters were frightened away. Revolted by the state's rhetoric and tactics, Chukovskaya went immediately to Pasternak to see how she could help. Six years later, in 1964, when Iosif Brodsky was put on trial for "parasitism,"* Akhmatova asked Chukovskaya to help organize support for him. Chukovskaya persuaded a number of highly respected writers to compose letters in his defense and her friend Frida Vigdorova traveled to Leningrad to make a transcript of the trial. Publication of this transcript abroad and its samizdat circulation at home produced such an outcry that Brodsky was released early from his term at a state farm in northern Arkhangelsk. Once he was back in Leningrad, however, no one could protect the poet from KGB harrassment, and in 1972 he was forced to leave the country.

In 1965 Andrei Sinyavsky and Yuli Daniel were arrested for publishing pseudonymously in the west. This time Chukovskaya herself wrote on their behalf, beginning a series of open letters she was to write during the late 1960s and early 1970s, some independently, some with others, defending writers, denouncing those who attacked them, insisting that the truth, no matter how unpleasant, must be revealed. They were collected and pub-

---

*Under Soviet law, every male over eighteen is required to work. Since Brodsky was not a member of the Writers' Union, his poetry writing did not legally qualify as work and he was subject to arrest for "parasitism."

lished later in Russian in New York as *The Open Word* (Otkrytoe Slovo, 1976), but none of them, of course, was printed in the Soviet Union. They circulated only in samizdat, while Chukovskaya's second novella, *Going Under* (Spusk pod vodu), published in the West in 1972 and in the major European languages soon thereafter, reached Soviet readers in "tamizdat," or bootleg western editions. Written in 1949–57, *Going Under* like *Sofia Petrovna* bears contemporary witness to Stalin's persecution of his own people, in this case writers and intellectuals, during the anti-Semitic campaign against "cosmopolitanism." The heroine of *Going Under* is trying to come to terms with the loss of her husband during the purges, and Chukovskaya struggles with her own sense of loss in *On this Side of Death* (Po etu Storonu Smerti), a collection of poems from her 1936–76 diaries which came out in Paris in 1978.

The Soviet authorities could not stop Lydia Chukovskaya from writing, but the moment Kornei Chukovsky died in 1969, they made her a literary pariah. Her books were removed from library shelves and her name forbidden to appear in print, excised even from photo captions in books about her father. Then on 9 January 1974, her de facto exclusion from publishing in the U.S.S.R. was made official: Chukovskaya was expelled from the Union of Writers. The direct cause was her 1973 article "The People's Anger," an analysis of the slander campaign against Andrei Sakharov and Alexander Solzhenitsyn in the Soviet press, but the step had become inevitable years earlier. In *The Process of Expulsion* (Protsess Iskluchenia, Paris, 1979), Chukovskaya explains that the constant compromise with conscience required of writers finally drove her into open opposition with the state. She tells of reaching a point when truth took her "by the throat" and "possessed [her] soul forever." She could no longer write with the censor in mind even if it meant no line of hers would ever again be published in her own country.

Chukovskaya's unwavering commitment to literary freedom is equaled only by her commitment to the memory of her father. Since Kornei Chukovsky's death in 1969, she has dedicated herself to preserving his cultural legacy. Determined not to lose the traces of that time in his life only she could remember, she wrote this lyrical reminiscence of childhood—a book still denied its rightful readership. With the help of her daughter and staunch friends, she has seen to the editing of his work and the cataloging of his large personal archive, and she turned the Chukovsky dacha at Peredelkino into a house-museum. Though the museum receives thousands of visitors a year, since 1976 it has been under legal attack from the Writers' Union, which wants to regain the property. Neighbors, friends, and admirers of Chukovsky have protested the Union's actions and made needed repairs when the Union would not. Chukovskaya has stood her ground and the museum continues to receive visitors from all over the country, but the appeals process, dragging on through the 1980s, has been a drain on her already failing health. She has suffered for a long time from a heart condition and, by the end of 1986, had become almost blind from cataracts. Until very recently, it seemed Chukovskaya was to remain embattled and officially mute for the rest of her life. As she entered her eightieth year, not a single line had been published under her name for twenty years, except for the fluke appearance of the first four chapters of *To the Memory of Childhood* described in the Afterword.* But 1987, a remarkable year in the Soviet Union, has brought unexpected improvement in Lydia Chukovskaya's situation. A series of cataract operations early in the winter restored partial vision in one eye; for the first time in years she can recognize faces and distinguish colors. In February the Writers' Union voted to rehabilitate Boris Pasternak, posthumously, as a mark of the new *glasnost*, or openness, in Soviet intellectual life. Chukovskaya was one of those invited to memorialize Pasternak on the anniversary of his death in May. Her appearance was greeted with a standing ovation and noted in the press, the first public mention of her name since 1969. Simultaneously several Soviet journals asked to publish excerpts from her Akhmatova diaries.

Chukovskaya refused. She insisted that nothing of hers could be published until *Sofia Petrovna*, the book the authorities had so long ago and suddenly rejected, had appeared in print. For months there was no response; then in September the Leningrad journal *Neva* announced publication of *Sofia Petrovna* for the first half of 1988. On the heels of this news came another pleasant surprise. An October article in the popular magazine *Ogonyok* described the Kornei Chukovsky house-museum as a national treasure, praised Lydia Chukovskaya's efforts to keep it going, and criticized the attempts by the Writers' Union to close it. For Lydia Chukovskaya the appearance of *Sofia Petrovna* fifty years after it was written and public, official support for the Peredelkino museum come as hard-won victories in a lifelong battle to safeguard memory and speak the truth.

---

*As this translation went to press, news came from Moscow that *To the Memory of Childhood* would be published in 1988 in the Soviet magazine *Semya* (Family).

Translator's Note

Bringing *To the Memory of Childhood* alive in English took the energy, wisdom, and commitment of many friends. A list, however incomplete, begins in Moscow with the author herself. Lydia Chukovskaya graciously granted permission for the project and devoted precious time to reviewing the translation with her own set of scrupulous readers there.

Here in the United States, Sarra Babyonyshev inspired the effort in the first place and remained mentor throughout. Natasha Pokrovsky, in Boston, and Jane Taubman, at Amherst, read the manuscript with wonderful care and consistently sound suggestions. In Chicago, Sasha Asarkan was a remarkable source of information on Russian culture, and Maria Zelvyansky provided much good advice on the Russian language. Frances and Jonathan Brent, through *Formations* magazine and the Northwestern University Press, welcomed the translation and with the steady help of Susan Harris transformed the manuscript into a book.

Many thanks to all of you and to my ever-supportive family.

Notes

Bracketed information has been provided by the translator.

Chapter III
1. Alexander Griboedov, "Woe from Wit," slightly adapted.
2. The letter has been lost.
3. Valery Bryusov, "The Meeting."

Chapter IV
1. "Childhood," from *The Life and Work of B.S. Zhitkov* (Moscow: Detgiz, 1955), 248.
2. From unpublished letters.

Chapter VI
1. Nikolai Nekrasov, "The Philanthropist."
2. Fyodor Tyutchev, "Oh what a wonder, you ocean at night."
3. Tyutchev, "Oh what a wonder . . . "
4. Alexander Pushkin, "The Bronze Horseman." Translated by Walter Arndt.
5. Kornei Chukovsky, *From Two to Five* (Moscow: Detskaya Literatura, 1970), 341-42.
6. Evgeny Baratynsky, "Piroskaf" (The Steamer). [Translated by Alexis.]
7. Alexander Blok, "Of valor, great deeds and fame . . . "
8. Nikolai Nekrasov, "The Funeral."
9. Nekrasov, "Silence."
10. Nekrasov, "The Return."
11. Yakov Polonsky, "On the fiftieth birthday of A.A. Fet."
12. Afanasy Fet.
13. I. Myatlev.
14. Pierre Beranger, "Le Petit Homme Gris," translated from the French by Vasily Kurochkin.
15. Nekrasov, "Ballet."
16. An 1860s satirical verse quoted by Herzen in his newspaper *Kolokol* (The Bell) in 1866. Author unknown.

Chapter VII

1. Boris Pasternak, "Mutiny at Sea," from *The Year 1905*.

Chapter VIII

1. Evgeny Baratynsky, "To the girl who in answer to the question: 'What's your name?' replied, 'I don't know.'"
2. Osip Mandelstam, "Ice Cream. Sun. Sponge Cake..." In *Poems* (Moscow-Leningrad: Gosudarstvennoye, 1928), 70.
3. Chukovsky, "Confessions of an Old Storyteller," *Literaturnaya Rossiya* (23 January 1970): 14.
4. Chukovsky, "On Children's Language," *To Mothers on Magazines for Children* (St. Petersburg: 1911), 103.
5. Chukovsky, "On Children's Language," 78.
6. Pushkin, "Poltava." [Translated by Walter Arndt.]
7. Pushkin, "October 19."
8. Pushkin, "To I.I. Pushchin." Translated by Walter Arndt.
9. Pushkin, "Farewell."
10. Nikolai Nekrasov, "On the Death of Shevchenko."
11. Mikhail Lermontov, "The Poet's Death."

Chapter IX

1. Bryusov, from his children's verses.
2. I.E. Repin, *Artistic Heritage*, vol. 2 (Moscow-Leningrad: AN SSSR, 1949), 370.
3. Blok, *Essays, Articles, Lectures*, vol. 2 (Moscow: GIKHL, 1955), 453.
4. Blok, *Essays, Articles, Lectures*, 456.
5. Anna Akhmatova, "Yes, I Loved Them, Those Evening Gatherings."
6. Blok, "The Artist."

Chapter X

1. Blok, "An angry glance from colorless eyes..." (the sixth poem in the "Carmen" cycle).
2. Vladimir Mayakovsky, "Ode to Judges."
3. Mayakovsky, "Ode to Judges."
4. Blok, "On the Railway."
5. Blok, "The Aviator."

Chapter XI

1. Chukovsky, "On Spiritual Illiteracy," *Literaturnaya Rossiya*, 12 July 1965.
2. Chukovsky, "On Children's Language," 101.
3. Unpublished letter to Ya. Grebenshchikov.
4. "Something about Young People," in *Diary of a Writer*.

Chapter XII

1. Chukovsky, "Confessions of an Old Storyteller," 14.
2. Chukovsky, "Literature and School," in *Collected Works*, vol. 6 (Moscow: Khudozhestvennaya Literatura, 1969), 596.

3. Pushkin, "The Hussar."
4. Pushkin, "The Hussar."
5. Pushkin, "The Bridegroom."
6. Pushkin, "Poltava."
7. Pushkin, "Bonaparte and the Montenegrans."
8. Chukovsky, "Literature and School," 592-93.
9. "The Goblet," Vasily Zhukovsky's Russian translation of the Friedrich Schiller ballad, "The Diver."

Chapter XIII
1. [The Russian verses are from "The Castle of Smaylho'me," Zhukovsky's translation of Sir Walter Scott's *The Eve of St. John*. For the English text I have used Scott, except for the lines where Chukovskaya's remarks hinge on the Zhukovsky text.]
2. [The passages from *Dombey and Son* are translated from Alexander Vvedensky's Russian version of the book, from which Chukovskaya was reading.]
3. *The Odyssey*, translated into Russian by Vasily Zhukovsky.
4. Anton Chekhov, *The Hero-Gentlewoman*. [The allusion is to a silly remark addressed to the long-suffering heroine by a foolish old general.]

Chapter XIV
1. Chukovsky, *Crocodile*.
2. Walt Whitman, "Roaming in Thought."
3. Chukovsky, *Dr. Ayboleet* (Dr. Ow-it-hurts). [Translated here as Dr. Help-me-please for reasons of rhythm and rhyme.]
4. Blok, "On Trial."
5. Pushkin, "Mozart and Salieri."
6. Nikolai Nekrasov, "Contemporaries" (Part II).
7. Pushkin, "Demons."
8. Nekrasov, "Hey, Ivan!"
9. A line from a poem by Alexei Pleshcheev, "Not a word, my friend, not a breath," which was set to music by Tchaikovsky.
10. Nekrasov, "Troika."

Chapter XVI
1. Repin, *Selected Letters*, vol. 2 (Moscow: Iskusstvo, 1969), 307–308.
2. Repin and V.V. Stasov, *Correspondence*, vol. 3 (Moscow-Leningrad, 1950), 36.
3. Chukovsky, "On Children's Language."
4. Chukovsky, *Voprosy Literatury* 1 (1972): 156
5. Olga Dyachkova, *Chukokkala*, 260.
6. Chukovsky, *Voprosy Literatury* 1, 169-70.
7. Chukovsky, *Voprosy Literatury* 1, 158.
8. Chukovsky, *Voprosy Literatury* 1, 162.

Chapter XVII
1. Repin, *Selected Letters*, vol. 2, 339-40.
2. Repin, *Selected Letters*, vol. 2, 357.

Afterword
1. Chukovsky, "Confessions of an Old Storyteller."
2. *Mayakovsky-Khudozhnik* (Mayakovsky the Artist) (Moscow: Sovietsky Khudozhnik, 1983), 30.
3. Chukovsky, *From Two to Five*. [An abridged English translation, which Chukovsky criticized, was published by the University of California Press in 1966.]

Biographical Glossary

Akhmatova, Anna Andreyevna (1889–1966): Major twentieth-century Russian poet. A member of the Acmeist group, she attained early fame, but was criticized as apolitical after the revolution. No new work of hers was published between 1922 and 1940, and in 1946 after a vitriolic propaganda campaign she was expelled from the Soviet Union of Writers. She and her poetry regained official status in the cultural thaw of the late 1950s, but *Requiem*, her tragic lament written during Stalin's purges, did not appear in print until 1987. She and Chukovskaya became friends in the 1930s and remained close until the poet's death in 1966. Chukovskaya's *Diary Notes on Anna Akhmatova* are the definitive record of the poet's life for the period they cover. Though they have not been published in the Soviet Union, the informed Soviet reader would understand the reference in Chapter X to the lesson her father taught her about recognizing the importance of her meetings with Akhmatova.

Andreev, Leonid Nikolaevich (1871–1919): Prose writer, dramatist, and publicist. Dealing candidly with social problems like sex and alcoholism, his short stories and allegorical plays were extremely controversial and popular at the turn of the century. He lived and dressed in a lavish, theatrical fashion. Though initially a supporter of revolution, he quickly became disillusioned, moving in November 1917 to his castle in Finland, where he soon died.

Babel, Isaac Emmanuilovich (1894–1941?): Popular short story writer from Odessa. His politically equivocal, erotically powerful tales, often with open Jewish subject matter, were widely read but met with mixed official response. He was arrested and his work confiscated in 1939, and after his rehabilitation in 1956, his widow was informed that he had died in prison.

Bakst, Leon (1866–1924): Artist and theatrical designer of World of Art group, known for set and costume design of *Les Ballets Russes*. Lived much of his life in France.

163

Baratynsky, Evgeny Abramovich (1800–1844): Lyric poet, contemporary and friend of Pushkin.

Blok, Alexander Alexandrovich (1880–1921): Leading symbolist poet and a major influence on the Russian poetry of his time. Despite his ambiguous, increasingly disillusioned view of the revolution, Blok has been canonized as a "great Soviet poet."

Bryusov, Valery Yakovlevich (1873–1924): Poet and critic, primary theoretician of symbolist school of poetry and editor of the literary journal *Vesy* (The Scales). Bryusov was one of the only symbolists to join the communist party and actively collaborate with the Bolsheviks.

Bunin, Ivan Alekseevich (1870–1953): Writer of prose and poetry, first Russian winner of Nobel Prize in Literature (1933). Lived in emigration in Paris after 1920.

Chaliapin, Feodor Ivanovich (1873–1938): Celebrated Russian operatic bass. Moved to the West in 1922.

Dobuzhinsky, Mstislav Valerianovich (1875–1957): Artist, theater designer, book illustrator. World of Art group. Emigrated in 1925.

Evreinov, Nikolai Nikolaevich (1879–1953): Playwright and director, historian and theoretician of the theater. Emigrated to Paris in 1920.

Fet, Afanasy Afanasievich (1820–92): Lyric poet. Believed in art for art's sake at a time when dominant critics felt literature should have didactic or ideological purpose.

Gogol, Nikolai Vasilyevich (1809–52): Leading nineteenth-century satirist, short story writer, novelist, and playwright.

Gorky, Maxim (1868–1936): Short story writer and novelist. Considered founder of socialist realism.

Gorodetsky, Sergei Mitrofanovich (1884–1967): poet and co-founder of Poets' Guild and Acmeist movement.

Grigoriev, Boris Dmitrievich (1886–1939): Expressionist artist of younger World of Art school.

Gumilyov, Nikolai Stepanovich (1886–1921): Acmeist poet and literary critic. Shot in 1921 for anti-Bolshevik conspiracy. First husband of Anna Akhmatova; they were divorced in 1918.

Herzen, Alexander Ivanovich (1812–70): Writer, journalist, and philosopher. Herzen's liberal ideas branded him a revolutionary and earned him internal exile in 1834 and 1840 in the conservative Russia of Nicholas I. After 1847 he decided to live in Europe, where he founded the emigre journal *Kolokol* (The Bell). His memoir *My Past and Thoughts* is a unique blend of reminiscence and political theory.

Ivanov, Vyacheslav Ivanovich (1866–1949): Symbolist poet and classical scholar. Established literary salon in Petersburg (1905) called *bashnya* (the tower). Emigrated to Italy in 1924.

Karamzin, Nikolai Mikhailovich (1766–1826): Poet, novelist, and historian. Introduced European-style sentimentalism to Russian literature. Authored twelve-volume *History of the Russian State.*. Major influence on Pushkin and his contemporaries.

Khlebnikov, Velimir (Victor Vladimirovich) (1885–1922): Futurist poet noted for experimentation with language. Led an eccentric, wandering life.

Khodasevich, Vladislav Felitsianovich (1886–1939): Poet, critic, and memoirist who emigrated to France in 1922. Unpublished thereafter in the U.S.S.R. until the era of *glasnost.*

Klyuchevsky, Vasily Osipovich (1841–1911): Historian noted for scrupulous research and documentation, author of standard Russian-language history of Russia.

Komissarzhevskaya, Vera Fyodorovna (1864–1927): Well-known actress and St. Petersburg theatrical personality.

Koni, Anatoly Fyodorovich (1844–1927): One of Russia's first modern jurists. A high-ranking magistrate, Koni had broad connections in the world of arts and letters, and his memoirs provide an excellent picture of contemporary cultural life.

Korolenko, Vladimir Galaktionovich (1853–1921): Humanist writer, critic, and social activist. A three-year exile in Siberia in the 1880s for populist activities provided much background for his fiction and non-fiction. He also battled in the press against such abuses as racial and religious discrimination, capital punishment, and police brutality.

Kulbin, Nikolai Ivanovich (1868–1917): St. Petersburg art critic and patron of avant-garde artists.

Kuprin, Alexsandr Ivanovich (1870–1938): Writer of novels and short stories depicting evils of society. Member with Gorky, Bunin, and Andreev of the Znanie (Knowledge) group.

Kuzmin, Mikhail Alekseevich (1875–1936): poet, prose writer, and playwright, author of *Wings*, one of the first novels with a homosexual theme published in Russia.

Lermontov, Mikhail Yurievich (1814–41): Romantic poet and novelist. He won both fame and exile for his poem "Death of a Poet," dedicated to Alexander Pushkin, and at age twenty-seven was shot in a duel himself.

Leskov, Nikolai Semyonovich (1831–95): Short-story writer, novelist, and journalist with a powerful grasp of idiomatic speech and an often satirical point of view.

Mandelstam, Osip Emilievich (1891–1938?): One of the greatest twentieth-century Russian poets. A member of the Poets' guild and an early Acmeist, he was arrested and sentenced to exile in 1934 for a poem about Stalin. He was arrested a second time in 1937 and died in Siberian transit camp sometime after 1938.

Marshak, Samuil Yakovlevich (1887–1964): Translator, poet, and children's writer, he edited the magazine *Novy Robinson* (The New Robinson) in 1924–25, and organized the children's section of the Leningrad State Publishing House, where Chukovskaya had her first job.

Mayakovsky, Vladimir Vladimirovich (1893–1930): Leader of futurist school of poetry, he became an active spokesman and propagandist for the new regime. His iconoclastic style, however, set him apart from the bureaucrats who ran the country, and his satirical plays, *The Bedbug* and *The Bathhouse*, indicate growing disillusionment. In 1930 he committed suicide, but later Stalin made him a cultural hero by declaring him "the best and most gifted poet of our Soviet epoch."

Meyerhold, Vsevolod Emilievich (1874–1940): Innovative theater director who also worked in opera and film. Though Meyerhold supported the communist system, Stalin found his art "formalistic" and had him sent to prison in 1939, where he died under torture.

Mussorgsky, Modest Petrovich (1839–81): Composer, best known for the operas *Boris Godunov* and *Khovanshchina*.

Nekrasov, Nikolai Alekseevich (1821–78): Poet, writer, and publisher, he wrote sympathetically about the oppressed Russian peasant at a time when stark realism was not considered appropriate for poetry. Kornei Chukovsky rediscovered and published many lines of Nekrasov's verse which had been lost or censored and wrote a comprehensive study of the man and his work, for which he received the Lenin prize in 1962.

Pasternak, Boris Leonidovich (1890–1960): Poet and novelist. His Nobel Prize for Literature in 1958 led to official censure, and Pasternak was forced to reject the honor. He has undergone a gradual rehabilitation since his death in 1960; his membership in the Writers' Union was restored in 1987 and *Dr. Zhivago* is to be published in the U.S.S.R. in 1988.

Polonsky, Yakov Petrovich (1819–98): lyric poet.

Puni, Ivan Albertovich (Jean Pougny) (1894–1956): Futurist painter and sculptor who emigrated to France.

Repin, Ilya Efimovich (1844–1930): Russian realist painter. Among the early members of the *Peredvizhniki* (Itinerants) group of painters who wished to develop their own, Russian style—as opposed to the conservative, European-influenced style of the academy—Repin became famous for his portraits and historical genre paintings. After the revolution, when Finland became a separate country, he decided to remain in Kuokkala rather than return to the Soviet Union.

Serov, Valentin Aleksandrovich (1865–1911): Realist artist and acclaimed portraitist.

Shevchenko, Taras Grigorievich (1814–61): Ukrainian national poet sentenced to ten years internal exile for his criticism of the nationalist policies of the Tsarist regime.

Shklovsky, Victor Borisovich (1893–1984): Literary critic, essayist, and novelist, leading member of the formalist movement.

Sologub, Fedor Kuzmich (1863–1927): Symbolist poet and writer.

Stanislavsky, Konstantin Sergeevich (1863–1938): Co-founder, Moscow Art Theater, actor, director, originator and teacher of the "Method" for actors.

Teffi, Nadezhda (pseudo. for Nadezhda Aleksandrovna Buchinskaya) (1872–1952): writer and poet, best known for comic-satiric work. Emigrated to Paris in 1920.

Tolstoy, Alexei Konstantinovich (1817–75): Poet and historical dramatist, known for his trilogy *The Death of Ivan the Terrible, Tsar Fyodor,* and *Tsar Boris.*

Tynyanov, Yuri Nikolaevich (1895–1943): Literary scholar and author of historical novels.

Tyutchev, Fyodor Ivanovich (1803–73): Lyric and philosophical poet.

Vigdorova, Frida Abramovna (1915–65): Writer, journalist, educator, and good friend of Lydia Chukovskaya. When poet Iosif Brodsky was tried for "parasitism" in 1964, Vigdorova took a shorthand transcript of the trial, which was later smuggled abroad.

Vrubel, Mikhail Aleksandrovich (1856–1910): Artist of World of Art group, known for intense, brooding images.

Zamyatin, Evgeny Ivanovich (1884–1937): Novelist, dramatist, critic. His 1924 novel *We,* first published in English and a precursor to George Orwell's *1984,* earned him vilification and he went into voluntary exile abroad in 1931. *We*'s first Soviet publication has been promised for 1988.

Zhukovsky, Vasily Andreevich (1783–1852): Poet and translator. Introduced Russia to romanticism with his translations of European ballads and narrative poetry. Tutor to the children of Tsar Nicholas I, friend and mentor to Pushkin and other writers and poets.

Zoshchenko, Mikhail Mikhailovich (1895–1958): Popular writer whose colloquial short stories poked fun at Soviet life. Attacked in 1946 for "vulgar parody," he was expelled with Akhmatova from the Writers' Union.